Developing Literate Mathematicians

A Guide for Integrating Language and Literacy Instruction into Secondary Mathematics

by

Wendy Ward Hoffer

More resources available online
www.nctm.org/more4u
Access code: DLM14522

NATIONAL COUNCIL OF
TEACHERS OF MATHEMATICS

Copyright © 2016 by
The National Council of Teachers of Mathematics, Inc.
1906 Association Drive, Reston, VA 20191-1502
(703) 620-9840; (800) 235-7566; www.nctm.org
All rights reserved

Library of Congress Cataloging-in-Publication Data

Hoffer, Wendy Ward.
  Developing literate mathematicians : a guide for integrating language and literacy instruction into secondary mathematics / by Wendy Ward Hoffer.
    pages cm
  Includes bibliographical references.
  ISBN 978-0-87353-728-5
  1. Mathematics—Study and teaching. 2. English language—Study and teaching.
  3. Language arts—Correlation with content subjects. I. Title.
  QA135.6.H64 2015
  510.71'2--dc23
                      2015016973

The National Council of Teachers of Mathematics is the public voice of mathematics education, providing vision, leadership, and professional development to support teachers in ensuring equitable mathematics learning of the highest quality for all students.

Printed in the United States of America

For my big sister,
Julianne Ward Nelson,
who came home from kindergarten every day
and taught me everything she had learned
and is teaching me still.

Only in the infinite do we find joy.

—Chandogya Upanishad

Contents

Accompanying Materials at More4U

For chapter 2:
Math Workshop Planning Template

For chapter 3:
Problem-Solving Scaffold
Math Workshop Planning Template: Teaching a Thinking Strategy for Math Reading

For chapter 4:
Vocabulary Instruction Planning Template

For chapter 5:
Discourse Planning Template

For chapter 6:
A Blueprint for Argument Writing

Preface

The purpose of this text is to offer you, a secondary mathematics teacher, insight into effective literacy instruction with concrete ideas for incorporating reading, writing, speaking, listening, and vocabulary learning in authentic ways into the weekly rhythm of your math courses. This book is not about starting over; rather, it is about efficiently and effectively layering intentional disciplinary literacy instruction into your already fine math teaching.

The first two chapters provide the big picture:

- Chapter 1 looks at why literacy is important to all learners and what literacy entails, and it offers an overview of disciplinary literacy in mathematics.

- Chapter 2 considers how teachers can apprentice students in new skills, literacy and others, through workshop model instruction, with mini-lessons to model thinking and extended student work time in which learners take responsibility for honing their mathematical and literacy skills.

The remaining chapters are devoted to the theory and practice of teaching specific components of literacy within a math workshop:

- Chapter 3: Reading
- Chapter 4: Vocabulary
- Chapter 5: Discourse
- Chapter 6: Writing

Most chapters include classroom examples, research summaries, sample lesson plans, graphic organizers, rubrics, and questions to ponder. Some planning templates and other materials are also available online for the reader's personal or classroom use; just go to nctm.org/more4u and enter the access code that appears on the title page of this book.

The conclusion ties up loose ends and offers some starting points for putting this work into practice.

How to Use This Book

Whether you are new to teaching or a veteran brushing up, this book can offer you a variety of practical ideas to implement right away. For best results, read it with a colleague or study group so that you can discuss the possibilities together, test-drive some, and report back on the outcomes. While I encourage you to read it from cover to cover, time may necessitate that you start someplace in the middle, perhaps exploring the vocabulary chapter first, to jump-start the year with some new word-learning routines. That approach will work, since each chapter can stand alone. My hope is that you eventually will find time to read all the chapters, so that your students can benefit from a balanced diet of literacy instruction integrated into their math learning.

About Me

When I first started teaching middle school math and science, I didn't know anything about literacy instruction, and I pretty quickly figured out that this was a problem. I found myself doing the darndest things: reading the math textbook aloud to the class; scratching wordy problems off the homework; wishing, when it came time for the state test, that I had done a better job teaching students to read and write as mathematicians. Here began my quest to understand the interrelationship between literacy and mathematics. I worked on teaching learners to read word problems, to write about graphs, and to talk through their thinking at the board, and soon the culture of my classroom—and the achievement of even my struggling students—began to shift. We all felt much more capable.

After a decade of working directly with students, I have spent the past ten years teaching teachers. I currently serve as Education Senior Director for the Denver-based Public Education & Business Coalition (PEBC), where my work often includes interpreting the organization's rich history in and deep knowledge of literacy instruction for my math and science teacher peers.

For a number of years, I designed and taught a graduate literacy course for Teach for America's secondary math and science teachers in Colorado. As an instructional coach, I devote time to observing in classrooms and coaching teachers; as a professor of math and science methods for preservice teachers in the Boettcher Teacher Residency, I explore with them how we can promote all learners' confidence and competence as mathematicians and scientists; as a designer of teacher professional development workshops, I strive to model and teach effective pedagogy in accessible ways. Through this work, I have gained a deep understanding of how we can best serve learners in their journey to make meaning of mathematics.

My previous books, *Science as Thinking: The Constants and Variables of Inquiry Teaching, Grades 5–10* (2009) and *Minds on Mathematics: Using Math Workshop to Develop Deep Understanding in Grades 4–8* (2012) offer practical approaches to teaching for understanding in each of those content areas. The book in your hands represents a synthesis of what I have learned and taught specifically about integrating literacy into secondary mathematics instruction.

Never was I more struck by the importance of drawing literacy instruction into mathematics teaching than when my own daughter, as a fifth grader, shoved her math homework at me across the breakfast counter, exclaiming, "I don't get this!" Nothing she knew about decoding text as a reader occurred to her when confronted with a word problem related to fractions. We talked through the need to read as a mathematician. No one had explained this to her, which did not surprise me, but I wished it had. Kids need us to help them understand—with explicit conversation—how the literacy skills that they already have apply in math, as well as—with explicit instruction—how to master the literacy unique to mathematicians.

As you embrace the challenge of becoming an exceptional math teacher by honing your craft as a literacy instructor, I invite you to take all the ideas and suggestions in this book and make them your own: Mix and match and modify them to meet your students' needs and your instructional purposes. If what you develop helps your students to read, write, and speak independently as mathematicians, understanding concepts and communicating ideas, you are feeding two birds—mathematics and literacy—with one piece of bread. I wish you and your students every success.

Acknowledgments

For bringing me to a place where I could write such a book, I gratefully acknowledge all my teachers, students, and colleagues, past and present, in schools and at the Public Education & Business Coalition. They have patiently coaxed me, a math and science teacher, into understanding how literacy instruction can be seamlessly integrated across the curriculum, as well as how one can engage adult learners in purposeful and meaningful work that translates into student growth.

In particular, I am grateful to Rosann Ward, for her wisdom and consistent support of my efforts to elevate educators; to Moker Klaus-Quinlan, for the brilliance, organization, and humor she brings to all our shared endeavors, especially the PEBC Math Institute, and for reminding me to take life bird by bird; to Annie Patterson, for all she has taught me about literacy and professional learning through our shared leadership of the Math and Science Study group and the Writing Seminars; as well as to other members of PEBC's Professional Learning Team—Michelle Morris Jones, Joyce Joyce, Dana Sorensen—for their excellence, efficacy, and reflectiveness; and to our Math Rodeo squad—Tracey Shaw, Sathya Wandzek, and Laurie Wretling—for continuing to challenge my thinking about what teachers need; and to PEBC's administrative and operations teams for backing us up wherever we go.

For opening their classroom doors and supporting my learning about what it means to teach mathematics effectively, I am grateful to all PEBC client schools and teachers, and especially to PEBC's math lab hosts—Deb Maruyama, Rachel Rosenberg, Kathy Sampson, and Tracey Shaw—for allowing me to learn with them and to include samples of their own and their students' work in this text.

For helping me to create the book in your hands, I am thankful to Suzanne Plaut, for getting me started with professional writing and being my developmental editor still; Myrna Jacobs at NCTM, for initiating this project; the EMC, for their feedback; Daniel Reinholz, for research assistance; John Ward, for his careful proofreading and thoughtful input; Stevi Quate, for her feedback; and Maxine Martin and Rose Hagood, for their help with final assembly.

I am deeply grateful to my children, who remind me every day what really counts.

And for Freedom, for all.

Introduction

As a math teacher, have you ever—

- Read a segment of a math textbook aloud to your class because you did not think students could understand it themselves?

- Cut sections out of a math problem set for being too verbose?

- Invited math learners to skip over tasks that required narrative responses because you did not think they could write like that?

- Rewritten math tasks to eliminate difficult vocabulary that you feared might stump students?

- Cringed at the amount of reading and writing expected of learners on standardized math assessments?

- Wished your students were more literate so that you could teach them more math?

If you can answer yes to any of these questions, this book is for you.

Let's face it: Mathematics learning requires tremendous literacy ability. Many of our students come to us without the reading, writing, speaking, listening, or vocabulary skills they need to progress, leaving math teachers asking themselves, "Do I give up time on my content to teach reading? Shouldn't they know how to write by now? Whose job is this literacy work anyway?"

Whose job is it? Yours. Math students do not learn to read or write or discuss ideas simply because we expect them to do so. Hope is not an instructional strategy. Literacy skills must be taught.

As a math teacher, you are a literacy instructor. You certainly are not the *only* literacy instructor; in fact, every content-area teacher is responsible for teaching the "disciplinary literacy" unique to her subject matter (see chapter 1 for more on this kind of advanced and specialized literacy). Yet as a math teacher, you have the unique and critical opportunity to support learners' achievement by teaching them what it means to read, write, speak, and think as mathematicians. A native in the land of mathematics, you most likely come by the disciplinary literacy skills of this content area with automaticity. By stepping back and recognizing what you know and can do as a literate mathematician and then teaching those skills explicitly to learners, you will enhance their capacity to make meaning for themselves of mathematics' vast landscape.

Being the Literacy Teacher Math Learners Need

Too often, when asked to attend literacy in-service workshops presented to the full faculty, math teachers sit at a back table and spend the hour or the day wondering how this work might relate to their own responsibilities in teaching math. I know this because often, after one of those "one size fits all" in-service events has flopped, I've been brought in and asked to talk with the math teachers to get them on board with schoolwide literacy initiatives.

And there is every reason that the math teachers *should* be on board with a focus on literacy: Literacy helps students learn math. Often, however, folks hold the misconception that literacy in mathematics would entail spending learning time writing haikus about fractions or reading Eratosthenes's geometrical treatises. Those activities would indeed be an appalling waste of time, given the incredible demands secondary math teachers face of ensuring that students have mastered a large body of content knowledge. When done well, content area literacy learning is not a tangent to content area learning but rather a complement to it.

To best promote student achievement, mathematics teachers need to understand and implement effective literacy instruction, which includes devoting time to explaining, modeling, practicing, and reflecting on the essential literacy skills—reading, writing, speaking, listening, and vocabulary—embedded in standards-based mathematics learning.

This may sound time-consuming. And initially it is. At first, we may see little evidence of students' progress in exchange for the effort we devote to disciplinary literacy. Yet persistence with literacy instruction can catalyze mathematical understanding at an exponential rate. In this book, we will visit classrooms where this has proven to be the case.

To be an effective mathematics instructor involves weaving together the warp of teaching literacy with the woof of teaching mathematics, attending to both in equal measure in service to students' gaining the whole cloth: mathematical understanding. Ultimately, we let go of considering ourselves either math teachers or literacy teachers, and consider our role as that of empowering learners to make meaning of the world. This ability, in fact, is the critical outcome of both literacy and mathematics teaching.

Math Matters

Children are marvels and deserve to be challenged and supported as such. When we structure our classes in ways that spur them to use their good minds well every day, we convey to each of them our confidence: "You are brilliant and capable, and productive struggle with the challenges of mathematics will make you stronger still. Through perseverance, effort, and imagination, all is possible for you."

Mathematics has come to be the proving ground that separates the AP students from the regular-track kids, the college bound from the high school graduates, the science majors from those who pursue the humanities, and, ultimately, it determines who will be the STEM professionals, those who will earn 26 percent more, on average, each year, than their non-STEM counterparts (Langdon et al. 2011). Math matters. A lot.

As a math teacher, you know how difficult it can be to inspire all learners to embrace and succeed in making meaning of mathematics. I hope that the resources in this book can serve as additions to your already rich toolbox, offering you new angles from which to leverage student understanding. Disciplinary literacy is a golden key that can unlock students' mathematics achievement.

Literacy for Mathematicians

It is not enough to have a good mind. The main thing is to use it well.

—René Descartes, *Discourse on Method*

Problems of the Day

- Why us?
- Why is literacy important?
- What is the relationship between literacy and disciplinary literacy?
- How do we develop literate mathematicians?

A colleague of mine attempted to go to the public library on March 31—Cesar Chavez Day—only to find it closed in Chavez's memory. She remarked on how appalled the civil rights activist would be by this "honor." Chavez himself understood the key role that literacy plays in promoting a just society; as he stated to the Commonwealth Club in San Francisco on Nov. 9, 1984, "Once social change begins, it cannot be reversed. You cannot un-educate the person who has learned to read. You cannot humiliate the person who feels pride. You cannot oppress the people who are not afraid anymore." As a teacher, you know that education in general—and literacy specifically—has the power to change lives.

Educators and policymakers, parents and teachers, want everyone to be literate. Literacy is the key to individual opportunity, a pillar of our democracy, and a responsibility of a civilized nation. But how exactly we define literacy, whose job it is to produce literate learners, and how we successfully coax a child from here to there can be more controversial. Simply put, literacy is the ability to make and communicate meaning. As teachers of any content area, it is indeed our role to support learners in meeting the literacy demands of our discipline. This book will offer you insight about how you can be an effective instructor of literacy in general and, more important, how you can support all learners in developing proficiency with the disciplinary literacy of mathematics.

Why Us?

Given our changing standards, math teachers are no longer able to focus exclusively on teaching mathematical concepts and are now expected to offer all learners explicit, embedded instruction in literacy. Astute mathematicians recognize that students' literacy is inherently linked to their mathematical success. Historian of mathematics Glen Van Brummelen of Quest University Canada describes the relationship between literacy and mathematics:

> I consider mathematics learning and literacy to be so closely aligned that they are insepara-
> ble. There are two main purposes to learning mathematics. The first is to learn how to think
> clearly and logically. It goes almost without saying that someone who cannot express ideas
> and reasoning clearly is very unlikely to be thinking clearly in the first place. In fact, one
> might even define mathematics to be the art of clear communication in the world of num-
> bers and geometry. The second purpose of learning mathematics is to be effective in quanti-
> tative and spatial relations when they arise in the physical world. In these cases, being able
> to solve a practical problem is entirely useless unless one is able to communicate it clearly to
> the target audience. (personal communication with the author)

Van Brummelen assures us of the intimate link between our content and literacy.

If only to multiply learners' mathematical prowess, if not to change the trajectory of their futures, math teachers are now called upon by the newest standards to integrate explicit literacy instruction into their regular math teaching routines—the specialized skills that students need to read, think, talk, and write as mathematicians.

In this chapter, we will articulate the nature and importance of literacy in general and then delve into the meaning of disciplinary literacy for mathematicians.

Why "General" Literacy Matters

As a mathematician, let the following statistics propel you to take up the charge of literacy instruction with gusto. Evidence clearly indicates that literacy has the power to save lives, transform the social order, and uplift a nation.

Literacy facilitates health

Literacy is a stepping-stone to school success and a prerequisite to high school graduation, which paves the way to healthy living. On average, high school graduates live longer, are less likely to become teen parents, and are more likely to raise healthier, better-educated children (Alliance for Excellent Education 2012).

By contrast, students who do not complete high school, often because of low literacy skills, encounter greater health challenges and incur significant costs. In a 2002 research review, medical professionals Andrus and Roth found that "forty-nine percent of patients with hypertension and 44% of patients with diabetes had inadequate functional health literacy" (Andrus and Roth 2002, p. 292). Colorado alone, according to statisticians' estimates, would save more than $280 million in health-care costs over the course of the lifetimes of each class of high school dropouts, had they earned their diplomas (Montelores Early Childhood Council 2013).

Illiterate individuals are at risk of poor health, may require expensive medical care, and might shorten their own lives because of their inability to understand doctors' instructions or follow written prescriptions.

Literacy promotes social justice

Literacy is a gateway to student achievement and high school graduation, yet literacy rates differ along racial lines. Longitudinal data produced by the National Assessment of Educational Progress (NAEP) demonstrates that, in reading, the achievement gap between white and black students and white and Hispanic students has narrowed since 1973. Still, in 2012, thirteen-year-old black students trailed their white peers by an average of 23 points, while Hispanic students scored 21 points below the average of their white counterparts (National Center for Education Statistics 2015).

Literacy is not the only predictor of high school graduation, but it is a significant factor. Nationwide, 70 percent of all students graduate from high school on time, yet the racial disparity in graduation rates is striking:

- 80 percent of Asian American students graduate from high school

- 76 percent of white students

- 58 percent of Latino students

- 53 percent of African American students

- 49 percent of Native American students (Alliance for Excellent Education 2012)

To close this achievement gap is to facilitate greater equality of opportunity for all children. A critical step in closing this gap is increasing the literacy rates of traditionally underperforming students. Literacy, therefore, is a social justice issue.

Speed Bumps on the Road to Literacy

How can it be possible that in a great modern nation such as ours, only 86 percent of our adult population is literate? There are a number of impediments that learners can encounter en route to full literacy, including—

- lack of access to books;

- parents' low literacy levels;

- dearth of literate role models;

- different language backgrounds;

- ineffective teachers or teaching methods;

- intellectual, physical, or emotional disabilities; and

- mismatch between learning styles and modes of instruction.

These are not excuses, just speed bumps some youngsters have to overcome. As teachers of all stripes, we can each work to decrease the possibility that hundreds of thousands of youth will continue to enter adulthood, year after year, ill-equipped to read the instructions on a bottle of medicine prescribed to save their mother's life, or their own.

Literacy creates individual opportunity

Literacy opens doors to individual economic opportunity. In 2011, the average annual income for a high school dropout was $25,100, as compared with $35,400 for a high school graduate, and $56,500 for those with a college degree (Baum, Ma, and Payea 2013). On average, in her lifetime, a college graduate today will earn $1 million more than a high school dropout.

Almost 85 percent of those tried in the juvenile court system are functionally illiterate; more than 60 percent of inmates of all ages are also functionally illiterate (Blankenship 2013). There is a positive correlation between illiteracy and crime, and a similar positive correlation between literacy and economic opportunity.

The nature of jobs is changing. While our grandparents' generation could earn good wages in stable manufacturing jobs with a high school diploma or less, the fastest-growing professions today have far greater than average literacy demands. Meanwhile, the fastest-declining professions have lower than average literacy demands. To be prepared for the jobs of the future, students need literacy skills.

Literacy promotes economic development

According to *The Economist* ("Counting Heads" 2004), a 1 percent increase in literacy scores leads to a 2.5 percent increase in labor productivity. Businesses in America currently spend upward of $60 billion annually on employee training, the greatest portion of which is devoted to remedial reading, writing, mathematics, and computer skills (ProLiteracy 2014). Supporting all learners in developing proficient literacy skills while in school will create far-reaching economic benefits: High school graduates are less likely to commit crimes, to depend on government health care, or to use public services such as housing assistance or food stamps. Economists estimate that cutting the nation's high school dropout rate in half would save the federal government $45 billion each year (Levin et al. 2006). Literacy is good for the economy.

Literacy learning, in general, is highly prized. Some students enter our math classrooms each year with basic literacy skills already in their backpacks, while others somehow missed picking them up along the way. As mathematics teachers attending to the literacy needs of learners, we not only enhance their mathematical understanding but also prepare them for lifelong success.

Literacy by the Numbers

Percent of U.S. adults who can't read	14%
Number of U.S. adults who can't read	32 million
Percent of U.S. adults who read below a fifth-grade level	21%
Percent of prison inmates who can't read	63%
Percent of high school graduates who can't read	19%

Source: National Center for Education Statistics 2013

> **Reflect**
>
> • What mathematical and literacy skills did you engage while reading these statistics about the importance of literacy?

What Is Literacy?

How do you define literacy for your students? What language skills do you believe they need to succeed in mathematics learning—and in life? As you review literacy standards authored by the National Council of Teachers of English as well as those by developed by the authors of the Common Core State Standards, I invite you to take this question personally, with a pen in hand: Underscore what you value and agree are key skills, and wrap parentheses around those you might leave to another teacher in another content area or year.

Literacy standards

The federal Workforce Investment Act of 1998 defined literacy as "an individual's ability to read, write, speak in English, compute and solve problems at levels of proficiency necessary to function on the job, in the family of the individual and in society" (Workforce Investment Act of 1998).

The National Council of Teachers of English (2013) defined literacy more broadly, asserting that twenty-first-century readers and writers need to—

- develop proficiency with the tools of technology;

- build relationships with others to pose and solve problems collaboratively and cross-culturally;

- design and share information for global communities to meet a variety of purposes;

- manage, analyze, and synthesize multiple streams of simultaneous information; and

- create, critique, analyze, and evaluate multimedia texts.

The Common Core State Standards Initiative, in the in the Common Core State Standards (CCSSI 2010), defines literacy even more globally and specifically. The Standards for English Language Arts state that students who are college and career ready will—

- demonstrate independence;

- build strong content knowledge;

- respond to the varying demands of audience, task, purpose, and discipline;

- comprehend as well as critique;

- value evidence;

- use technology and digital media strategically and capably; and

- come to understand other perspectives and cultures.

To this end, the Common Core's authors made an explicit effort to delineate how literacy instruction ought to be integrated across all content areas by articulating a separate set of literacy standards for history/social studies, science, and technical subject teachers, as described briefly in figure 1.1. Holding the broad goals on the preceding page as a backdrop, the majority of this book focuses on the specific components of literacy as defined by the Common Core: reading, writing, speaking, listening, and language.

Common Core literacy shift	In math, students . . .
Regular practice with **complex texts** and their academic language	• read nonfiction from textbooks, peers' work, or other resources • learn and use mathematical vocabulary
Reading, writing, and speaking **grounded in evidence from texts**, both literary and informational	• read, write, and discuss ideas and solutions • use evidence and argument to evaluate and respond to the thinking of others
Building knowledge through content-rich nonfiction	• read complex nonfiction chock-full of abstract concepts and challenging vocabulary

Fig. 1.1. Math learning aligned with Common Core (CCSSI 2014) literacy shifts

Disciplinary Literacy

With accountability to so many standards and responsibility to all our students, math teachers are wise to home in on what literacy instruction really ought to look and sound like in our classrooms. So, let us zero in now on the traditional domains of literacy—reading, writing, and speaking—which allow us access to all the higher-order opportunities required for college and career readiness as described by the Common Core.

Researchers Timothy and Cynthia Shanahan (2008) describe literacy learning as including three layers:

- Basic literacy: literacy skills such as decoding and knowledge of high-frequency words that underlie virtually all reading tasks

- Intermediate literacy: literacy skills common to many tasks, including generic comprehension strategies, common word meanings, and basic fluency

- Disciplinary literacy: literacy skills specialized to history, science, mathematics, literature, or other subject matter

Elementary school teachers devote a great deal of instructional time to ensuring that learners achieve basic and intermediate literacy skills. Yet explicit content-area literacy instruction often drops off abruptly in middle and high school, just as students are expected to comprehend and compose more technical texts written with complex academic language in content-specific genres. Accessing and responding to these specialized texts often requires specialized literacy skills unique to the content area, yet few content-area teachers invest time and energy in developing students' disciplinary literacy.

"Because students do not usually enter content-area classrooms knowing how to read and write the specialized print and non-print texts of the various disciplines, teachers must provide literacy instruction in content-area classrooms," Tom Bean explains in the foreword to (Re)Imagining Content-Area Literacy Instruction (Draper 2005, p. 2).

Timothy and Cynthia Shanahan (2008) go on to describe the nature of high-quality content-area literacy instruction: It is authentic to the discipline, and it cultivates learners' true literacy in that content area.

Disciplinary literacy includes an understanding of the ways knowledge is created and shared within a discipline, as well as an understanding of the texts and discourse used by that discipline. For mathematics teachers, disciplinary literacy instruction begins with understanding what it means to read, write, speak, and listen as a mathematician. Shanahan and Shanahan (2008, p. 52) provided this example of how mathematicians read:

> When one of the mathematicians was thinking aloud during the reading of a journal article, he explained that one of the first things he did when reading was to memorize the variables that were to be used in the rest of the article. Even though the article began as mostly prose, he would soon be reading only symbols, and he did not want to interrupt his flow of thought by having to return to the definitions.

This example, unique to the content area of mathematics, illustrates a specialized reading skill unlikely to be introduced in any other course. So as content-area teachers, we can both continue to develop students' basic and intermediate literacy skills and build on those by offering direct instruction in disciplinary literacy.

Essentially, the work of the Shanahans and their colleagues illuminates the reality that literacy is learned in layers, that the literacy of each subject area is unique, and that as content teachers our role is to support learners by intentionally introducing them to the complexity and nuances of literacy as it applies to our chosen discipline. A study of the writing of professionals in our content area will help us gain insight into the genres of disciplinary writing; eavesdropping on the discussions of professional engineers, mathematicians, statisticians, accountants, and economists at work will assist us in identifying key features of mathematical discourse, as we will do later in this book.

The disciplinary literacy of mathematics

> *Disciplinary literacy* is based on the premise that students can develop deep conceptual knowledge in a discipline *only* by using the habits of reading, writing, talking, and thinking which that discipline values and uses.
>
> —McConachie et al., "Tasks, Text, and Talk: Literacy for All Subjects"

Knowing that literacy is a cornerstone of lifetime achievement, that literacy involves many modes of communication, and that literacy must be taught in each discipline throughout a student's career in school, let us look closely at the disciplinary literacy of mathematics.

Disciplinary literacy can be considered as the means by which students engage with and learn new material, as well as the ways in which they demonstrate their understanding of it. Reflecting on your own experience as a math learner in school, you probably recollect numerous ways that you were expected to rely on your literacy skills both to learn content and to present your learning: reading the text, explaining a solution, writing a proof, and so forth. Can you recall ever being explicitly taught how to do so? Disciplinary literacy requires more than assigning literacy tasks in the context of math teaching. Rather, it needs to evolve to incorporate direct instruction about what these literacy skills are and how we can harness their power to generate mathematical understanding.

Mathematics and Literacy through History

Mathematics learning is a journey of understanding. To understand is to make knowledge one's own, readily available for application in new circumstances. Mathematics and literacy are and have always been symbiotic. The earliest mathematical understandings were shared in spoken words. The first geometric discoveries were documented in written treatises.

The early history of mathematics is known by its texts: notched animal bones, carved clay tablets dried in the sun. Greek, Chinese, and Indian mathematicians left us centuries-old evidence of their thinking in books, on cloth or parchment. We know that the early centers of learning, such as Plato's fourth-century academy, engaged mathematicians in great debates. Vast libraries could be filled with the mathematical texts of earlier civilizations, and Euclid's textbook, *The Elements,* at 2300 years old, still forms the basis for introductory geometry courses today. Text and conversation have always been the means to mathematical understanding.

Presently, professional mathematicians, as well as the vast array of professionals who use mathematics in their work, rely on their literacy skills to learn, to share, and to teach. Just take one look at the seven Millennium Prize Problems (posed by the Clay Mathematics Institute in 2000 with a $1 million reward for the solution to each) for a glimpse into what professional-level literacy entails for mathematicians. Mathematics learning is difficult. Yet without literacy, it is nigh impossible.

Our students, as mathematicians, require instruction in the disciplinary literacy of mathematics to succeed. As math teachers, we must therefore allow time and space for direct instruction and rehearsal of literacy skills in service of content learning targets.

Disciplinary literacy in this book

Let us now consider broadly what literacy in mathematics includes (subsequent chapters will address each of the following strands in greater depth):

- Reading: Making sense of a variety of genres for multiple purposes—prose, problems, diagrams, graphs, equations, proofs, models, solutions, or justifications (chapter 3)

- Vocabulary: Learning and using, understanding and remembering mathematical vocabulary; being able to use root words to make sense of new, unknown terms (chapter 4)

- Discourse: Engaging in purposeful conversations about mathematical ideas, speaking and listening about concepts, solutions, errors, strategies (chapter 5)

- Writing: Composing mathematical texts in a variety of formats to explain solutions, analyze errors, and reflect on learning experiences (chapter 6)

All these aspects of literacy can naturally be encompassed within learners' mathematical experience, and you may already be asking students to engage with most on this list. Although for the purpose of this text the four areas of literacy described above have been separated, we know that they are, in fact, inextricably linked, interconnected as part of each learner's web of meaning making. Simply for the purpose of explanation, we artificially tease them apart.

The purpose of this book is to offer you strategies that invite students not only to have literacy experiences while learning math but also to learn and master the literacy skills needed by successful mathematicians.

Literacy in Any Language

In my home state of Colorado, the number of students whose first language is not English has grown by nearly 300 percent in the past decade (Klaus-Quinlan and Nathenson-Mejía 2010), and our state is certainly not unique. Many students are challenged to master mathematics content while also developing second language skills. In these cases, students can benefit from exercising their literacy in their native language and using it as a tool for mathematics learning. More critical than that they discuss their mathematical ideas in English is that they discuss them at all.

Research describes the value to learners of code-switching, changing back and forth from one language to another:

> It is important for analyses of bilingual mathematical conversations to avoid interpreting code switching as a deficiency and instead explore how code switching can be a resource for mathematical communication. Sociolinguistics research suggests that we should not expect bilingual students to switch into their first language only to provide a missing English vocabulary term. While some students may sometimes use their first language in this way, other students will use their first language to explain a concept, justify an answer, describe mathematical situations or elaborate, expand and provide additional information. . . . In general, code witching has been documented as a resource for elaborating on a point that is repeated, without repeating the initial utterances word for word. In particular, code switching can provide resources such as phrases from the mathematics register in two languages and multiple ways to participate in mathematical discourse practices. (Moschkovich 2007, p. 18)

Mathematical talk, therefore, need not be limited by English proficiency. To discuss ideas in any language is to develop both literacy and understanding.

Developing literate mathematicians is best done in the context of workshop-model instruction, where the bulk of students' learning time is devoted to reading, problem solving, discussing, and writing as mathematicians. A workshop allows time for students to build their agency through tasks that engage them in productive struggle in a community of learners with whom they collaborate in the development of rich mathematical understanding. In chapter 2, we will explore this instructional approach in greater detail.

Disciplinary literacy in the NCTM Mathematics Teaching Practices

Principles to Actions, published by the National Council of Teachers of Mathematics (NCTM) in 2014, articulates a short set of descriptors of effective instruction—the Mathematics Teaching Practices—known to enhance math learning at all grade levels. Figure 1.2 helps us examine how each of those teaching practices is linked with literacy. Chapter references are included in the right-hand column; further detail on how to implement each strategy is included later in the text.

NCTM Mathematics Teaching Practice	Opportunity to integrate disciplinary literacy instruction
Establish mathematics goals to focus learning. Effective teaching of mathematics establishes clear goals for the mathematics that students are learning, situates goals within learning progressions, and uses the goals to guide instructional decisions.	Along with content learning goals, establish process goals for daily math workshops that include reading, writing, speaking, and listening about mathematics (chapter 2).
Implement tasks that promote reasoning and problem solving. Effective teaching of mathematics engages students in solving and discussing tasks that promote mathematical reasoning and problem solving and allows multiple entry points and varied solution strategies.	Explicitly teach learners the **reading** strategies they need to make sense of word problems and complex mathematical texts and tasks (chapter 3). Offer instruction and support for the development of **discourse** skills required to engage in mathematical discussions (chapter 5).
Use and connect mathematical representations. Effective teaching of mathematics engages students in making connections among mathematical representations to deepen understanding of mathematics concepts and procedures and in using tools for problem solving.	Support learners in making sense of multiple representations by teaching the **reading** skills needed to understand surface and deep structures of varied text (chapter 3).
Facilitate meaningful mathematical discourse. Effective teaching of mathematics facilitates discourse among students to build shared understanding of mathematical ideas by analyzing and comparing student approaches and arguments.	Scaffold learners' ability to engage in respectful, meaningful mathematical **discourse** and in collaborating with peers (chapter 5).

Fig. 1.2. Integrating literacy instruction into NCTM's (2014) Mathematics Teaching Practices

Pose purposeful questions. Effective teaching of mathematics uses purposeful questions to assess and advance students' reasoning and sense making about important mathematical ideas and relationships.	Invite learners to respond effectively both **orally** (chapter 5) and in **writing** (chapter 6) as a means of synthesizing their thinking.
Build procedural fluency from conceptual understanding. Effective teaching of mathematics builds fluency with procedures on a foundation of conceptual understanding so that students, over time, become skillful in using procedures flexibly as they solve contextual and mathematical problems.	Support learners in articulating problem solving strategies in **written** form (chapter 6). Develop conceptual understanding with rich **vocabulary** instruction (chapter 4).
Support productive struggle in learning mathematics. Effective teaching of mathematics consistently provides students, individually and collectively, with opportunities and supports to engage in productive struggle as they grapple with mathematical ideas and relationships.	Provide specific scaffolds for literacy challenges with explicit mini-lessons and opportunities to reflect during math workshop (chapters 2, 3, 4, 5, 6).
Elicit and use evidence of student thinking. Effective teaching of mathematics uses evidence of student thinking to assess progress toward mathematical understanding and to adjust instruction continually in ways that support and extend learning.	Through **workshop-model** instruction (chapter 2), offer learners the means to communicate their thinking, progress, and growth, **orally** (chapter 5) and in **writing** (chapter 6).

Fig. 1.2. *Continued*

Responsibility for Literacy

If this all feels a bit overwhelming at this stage, take heart. As a content-area teacher, you are a member of a cross-curricular team of teachers, each of whom is chipping away at the challenges and working toward the literacy standards from her own angle. So rather than feel burdened by the plethora of literacy learning targets you are now explicitly expected to ladle into your lessons, try looking on that list as a buffet, not a fixed menu. The next chapter will explore how workshop-model instruction can support you and your students in digesting your literacy selections efficiently, without sacrificing content learning.

So, ask yourself: Which aspects of literacy instruction would best serve my students? What could I authentically tackle in the context of our math learning this year? Take up your answer to that question as your charge in moving forward, and feel confident that by doing this, you are doing enough. Students have many content teachers and more years in school to master the craft of disciplinary literacy, and, with your help, they will.

"Yeah, but . . . "

- *"It's not my job to teach literacy—just math."*

Math learning and literacy learning have always been interdependent. Historically, math teachers have instructed students only on the former, yet what we know now is that when we also add direct instruction in the latter, students learn more math. When we include disciplinary literacy as an integral part of our math instruction, we are better math teachers.

- *"If I teach literacy, I will run out of time to cover my content."*

Literacy instruction does take time but also enhances learners' understanding. Our role as math teachers is to support students in developing that understanding, rather than hurrying them through the chapters.

- *"My students will get mad if I make them read and write in math class."*

Unfortunately, modern schooling has perpetuated the myth that the subjects are all separate, that there is to be no singing in science and no muckraking in math. To help learners rethink this misconception, we can describe for them the value of integration between content areas: We use timelines to help us understand history, graphs to make sense of science, fractions to interpret musical notation, so why not writing to support us as mathematicians?

Apprenticing Mathematicians in a Workshop

If there is no struggle, there is no progress.

—Frederick Douglass, "West India Emancipation" speech, August 1857

Problems of the Day

- How can we cultivate learners' mathematical thinking?
- How can we design and facilitate effective math workshops?

Every once in a while, I dream back to my high school calculus courses. I can still hear the rattling sound of our teacher energetically chalking symbols on the slate at the front of the room. He would spend the majority of fifty minutes at the board working conic sections and integrals with aplomb. We copied down everything he wrote. Once in while, he would holler at someone to tell him what to do next. I always sat in the same seat, second row, third back, where I sometimes ducked behind the big boys who liked to sit up front and be called on, but I would get hollered at anyhow, and would have to cough up a derivative or a domain, either to be scolded or praised—I was often unsure which to expect. We learned math by copying.

When the AP exam presented us with big blank sheets of paper on which to scrawl solutions all our own, I remember desperately wishing I understood more about what all the symbols represented and which I was meant to put where. Despite my long years as a devoted mathematical spectator, I had yet to grasp the underlying point. During the exam, I wrestled to combat an existential crisis: Why were we doing this?

Why Math Workshop?

The purpose of teaching and learning mathematics is understanding. When we understand, we can remember, transfer knowledge to new contexts, apply concepts to novel situations, look at problems from varied perspectives, and explain in ways that make sense to others. Though this was not my initial experience as a calculus learner, that course did propel me to recognize the importance of understanding, the need that I—and all students—have to develop strategies that will help us to make meaning of mathematics for ourselves.

To that end, a math workshop is an ideal forum for learners to construct their own mathematical understanding through rich interactions with both content and peers, in line with Lev Vygotsky's (1978) theory of social constructivism. The big idea behind a math workshop is that whoever is doing the majority of the speaking, solving, justifying, and explaining is doing the learning; since our purpose is to teach students math, our workshops need to be about students doing the work of mathematicians. In a workshop, learners are actors, not audience members, and teachers are coaches, not sages. A math workshop is a structure that turns over the work of learning math—and the responsibility for doing so—to students.

A classic workshop, lasting the length of one period of math, offers discrete opportunities in every lesson or learning sequence for direct instruction or modeling (mini-lesson), the majority of time devoted to students' independent and small-group work on rich tasks (work time), and a final segment for synthesis, metacognition, and formative assessment (reflection). Recent research on math reform demonstrates such approaches to be especially powerful when applied in heterogeneous groups (Boaler and Foster 2014). Though the workshop structure is flexible, the ritual of workshop is a powerful way to consistently convey to students that their work and their thinking are the primary focus of learning time.

Learners thrive in a math workshop when they are apprenticed as capable, independent problem solvers. Workshop-model instruction affords learners the time to experience, not just to observe, all eight Mathematical Practices detailed by the Common Core State Standards. In order to, first, "Make sense of problems and persevere in solving them," students need opportunities to face challenges and experience the productive struggle called for by NCTM's Mathematics Teaching Practices. Workshop is the cauldron of mathematical grappling. We set learners up with challenges, support their progress, and together look back on all they achieved and came to understand.

Learners can tackle more challenging problems collaboratively than they could independently; their comprehension is catalyzed by hearing the thinking of their peers. For this reason, discourse—engaged, accountable conversations about mathematical content—plays a key role in a math workshop. Discourse affords learners opportunities to reason, argue, and critique the thinking of others. Students need training and skilled facilitation to develop their capacity for generative conversations, and we know from international comparative studies of classroom practice that discussing mathematical ideas and defending them promote students' mathematical understanding. (Discourse is discussed further in chapter 5.)

Workshop-model literacy instruction was popularized by Donald Graves (1983) as a structure to support young writers. Literacy teachers soon embraced workshops for reading as well, with many using this forum for teaching and practicing thinking strategy instruction. Presently, teachers across all content areas are exploring the value of workshop-model instruction as a vehicle to engage and inspire students to own their learning; I described this approach in great detail in my book *Minds on Mathematics: Using Math Workshop to Develop Deep Understanding in Grades 4–8* (2012).

Workshop-model math instruction affords teachers the space and time to enact the research-based recommendations of the National Research Council's synthesis *Adding It Up*:

namely, when planning and facilitating a workshop, we can "select cognitively demanding tasks, plan the lesson by elaborating the mathematics that the students are to learn through those tasks, and allocate sufficient time for the students to engage in and spend time on the tasks" (Kilpatrick, Swafford, and Findell 2001, p. 9).

In mathematics classrooms, the workshop structure is a powerful routine within which teachers can model the thinking and discourse of mathematicians, invite students to engage in rich problem solving, and then reflect on how their thinking and self-efficacy grows and changes. In this chapter, we will further explore the structure and purpose of math workshop in general, as well as examine how it can offer openings for the appropriate integration of literacy learning.

A Typical Math Workshop

Stepping into class, students know to pull out their notebooks and begin work on the problem of the day projected on the screen:

> Sarah lives $3/4$ of a mile from school. She walks $1/2$ of the way, then rides the bus. How far does she walk?

After a few minutes of silent work, students are invited to pair and share and then come together as a learning community to discuss their solutions. This opening activates the group's curiosity about how to calculate $1/2$ of $3/4$.

After a few minutes of discussion, Mrs. Naylor introduces her sixth graders to the learning targets of the day:

- Content: Understand how to calculate a fraction of a fraction.

- Process: Explain with multiple representations (calculations, pictures, and writing) why a solution is or is not accurate.

Then she presents her mini-lesson, critiquing an incorrect solution to the Sarah problem. She thinks aloud about how that author came to the conclusion that Sarah had walked $1/2$ of a mile, rather than $1/2$ of the $3/4$ mile, and then on the interactive whiteboard represents her own accurate solution arithmetically and with a sketch. She writes a few sentences about why her answer is accurate, and the misconception that led the other author astray. Before students turn to their own error analysis task, they review the steps their teacher took in her work:

- Review the solution given.

- Solve the problem yourself and represent your thinking with numbers and pictures.

- Decide whether you agree.

- Explain why or why not in sentences.

A Typical Math Workshop, *continued*

During work time, students are presented with a peer's inaccurate solution to a related but different problem:

> Troy's gas tank is $2/3$ full. He uses $1/4$ of the remaining gas to drive to work. What will the gas gauge read when he arrives?

The solution given was $5/12$, and students were asked to analyze whether this was correct or not, and why.

In table groups, learners puzzled, discussed, compared, and crafted solutions with illustrations and sentences of explanation, which they shared under the document camera during the last segment of the workshop. In closing, students were asked to reflect on what is important to remember when calculating a fraction of a fraction. These written reflections, along with learners' completed work, served as fodder for their teacher's planning of the next day's workshop.

Workshop-model instruction is supported by research

Research on student learning supports the practice of workshop-model instruction. In the synthesis *How People Learn,* the National Research Council identified "active learning" as a key factor in student success: "A 'metacognitive' approach to instruction can help students learn to take control of their own learning by defining learning goals and monitoring their progress in achieving them" (Bransford, Brown, and Cocking 2000, p. 14). Further, in describing how research can inform classroom instruction, the National Research Council emphasizes the importance of the following:

- Learner-centered schools and classrooms

- Knowledge-centered instruction, which includes models of mastery

- Regular, formative, learner-friendly assessments

- Community-centered learning experiences

Each of these features is inherent in the workshop model. Within a math workshop, the structure serves as a forum for differentiation and individualized instruction, offers teachers opportunities to share exemplars, creates time for frequent communication about students' progress, and brings the group together each day as a learning community to share and reflect on their mathematical thinking and understanding.

Workshop-model instruction offers a context for teachers to enact mathematics instructional practices demonstrated effective by the TIMSS Video Study (Hiebert, Stigler, and Manaster 1999), which compared mathematics learning experiences of eighth graders in three countries—Germany, Japan, and the United States. This study assessed the amount of time spent on practicing routine procedures, applying procedures to new situations, or thinking up new procedures. Researchers found that typical American students, the lowest achievers among those in the three nations in the study, spent 95.8 percent of their time practicing routine procedures, in stark contrast to Japanese students, who spent only 40 percent of their time on this and 44 percent of their time on inventive thinking. Practicing routine procedures offers limited scope for the kinds of conversation invited by the Common Core, yet a workshop model offers an ideal frame for learners to engage in inventive thinking with well-facilitated tasks of high cognitive demand.

Metacognition in a Workshop

Stopping to think carefully about things, to reflect, is almost sure to result in establishing new relationships and checking old ones. It is almost sure to increase understanding. (Hiebert 1997, p. 5)

Simply put, metacognition describes the thinking we each do about our own thinking. Metacognition promotes student engagement, deepens understanding, and leverages achievement (Hattie 2009). Integral to the structure of a workshop are opportunities to invite student metacognition: We begin with a purpose. Why are we doing what we are doing, and why should each learner care? Then throughout work time, we ask learners to attend to their own progress and address misconceptions or confusion by drawing on the resources in the classroom: peers, texts, tools, instructors. The final segment of a classic workshop, Sharing and Reflection, is yet another opportunity for learners to activate their self-awareness: How is my mathematical thinking similar to or different from that of my peers? What mathematical concepts do I understand now that I did not grasp before? What do I need to feel confident that I have mastered this content? Metacognition of this sort, whether brief or in depth, woven throughout learners' experience, serves to sustain investment as well as promote the sort of self-awareness we all need to succeed.

Math workshop fosters NCTM Mathematics Teaching Practices

Within a workshop, teachers are easily able to implement all eight of the Mathematics Teaching Practices recommended by NCTM, as described in figure 2.1. This table offers a mere summary of connections that will be illuminated later in the chapter.

NCTM practice	Relationship to workshop
Establish mathematics goals to focus learning.	Each workshop focuses on a specific learning target, presented in the mini-lesson. In addition to content learning targets, we can include process targets referring to the NCTM Mathematics Teaching Practices or the CCSS Literacy Standards.
Implement tasks that promote reasoning and problem solving.	The bulk of work time in a workshop is devoted to students collaborating on cognitively demanding, in-depth tasks that elicit their mathematical thinking. Teachers prepare students for this work by modeling thinking and problem solving during the mini-lesson. One cannot conduct a workshop with a typical worksheet.

Fig. 2.1. Implementing NCTM's (2014) Mathematics Teaching Practices in a workshop

NCTM practice	Relationship to workshop
Use and connect mathematical representations.	Workshops afford ample work time for learners to engage in rich problems and to explore various mathematical representations. Students share and discuss representations, make connections among different approaches, and develop conceptual understanding.
Facilitate meaningful mathematical discourse.	Discourse is a key attribute of workshops. While learners do benefit from some solo problem solving, the majority of work time in a math workshop is given to collaborative problem solving and then discussion of approaches and solutions.
Pose purposeful questions.	While students are engaged in the work time of a workshop, teachers are free to confer with individuals and small groups about their thinking, asking probing questions to deepen understanding.
Build procedural fluency from conceptual understanding.	Workshop-model math instruction focuses on developing conceptual understanding by engaging learners in tasks that lift up key mathematical ideas. Conceptual understanding built within a workshop can be enhanced with follow-up or homework tasks designed to facilitate procedural fluency.
Support productive struggle in learning mathematics.	In cooperation with peers, students devote their work time to challenging tasks that draw on their mathematical thinking and reasoning. Teachers support productive struggle by presenting important information during the mini-lesson, conferring with groups, and, as needed, catching the entire class's attention to provide additional support.
Elicit and use evidence of student thinking.	Students' thinking is the central focus of all conversation in a workshop. Teachers listen more than they speak and invite peers to respond to the thinking of their classmates to advance discussion and understanding during sharing and reflection.

Fig. 2.1. *Continued*

Math workshop addresses the Common Core

While some math teachers puzzle over how to integrate all eight of the Common Core Standards for Mathematical Practice (shown in fig. 2.2), others have found that a workshop is the answer to this dilemma. Within the context of a well-designed and effectively facilitated workshop, learners can experience all of these mathematical practices seamlessly, exploring and solving carefully selected, rich problems; engaging in collaboration and discourse with their peers; and generating deep mathematical understanding as a result.

Challenged with higher-order tasks and engaged as a community of learners solving them, students in a workshop experience abundant problem-solving opportunities, where they make sense, reason, and model, and they encounter numerous chances to argue, critique, and strategize with tools. Engaged in discourse about their work, learners support one another in attending to precision, finding the structure, and reasoning within a challenge. Yet a workshop needs to be built around a juicy task, one that offers multiple entry points, invites several possible approaches, and presents some ambiguity to be addressed.

Some teachers express concern about spending significant time on a small number of rich tasks, worried about how this approach will affect their pacing and content coverage. Yet research tells us that time spent understanding fewer problems more deeply is more efficient in advancing student learning than simply completing more work.

---

1. Make sense of problems and persevere in solving them.

2. Reason abstractly and quantitatively.

3. Construct viable arguments and critique the reasoning of others.

4. Model with mathematics.

5. Use appropriate tools strategically.

6. Attend to precision.

7. Look for and make use of structure.

8. Look for and express regularity in repeated reasoning.

Fig. 2.2. Common Core Standards for Mathematical Practice (CCSSI 2010)

Math workshop fosters students' disciplinary literacy

Within the frame of math workshops, opportunities to promote students' literacy as mathematicians are abundant. During mini-lessons, students can document new vocabulary learning in writing as well as engage in discourse. Throughout work time, discourse continues, and learners are also engaged as readers, writers, and problem solvers. Sharing and reflection again focus on discourse, integrating discipline-specific vocabulary, and learners again document their thinking in writing.

Within a math workshop, literacy is naturally integrated as a means to scaffold meaningful conversation and record and respond to mathematical ideas. Students who learn math within a workshop structure—in which they grapple with challenges, discuss ideas, justify solutions, and defend their thinking—will be better prepared not only to succeed academically but also to develop the life skills necessary to excel.

For all learners, especially English language learners, scaffolded literacy opportunities integrated into a workshop not only build their academic language and disciplinary skills but also deepen content understanding and promote achievement (Zwiers 2006, 2007).

Math workshop develops internationally competitive students

As described above, the TIMSS video study illuminated the need for American math learners to devote more math learning time to rich, in-depth problem-solving tasks. For U.S. teachers keen to increase rigor and engagement in math, workshop-model instruction can provide just the forum. Within a workshop, students are thinking as mathematicians. Challenged to collaborate to solve problems, compare ideas, and understand peers' thinking, learners hone twenty-first-century skills: creativity and innovation, critical thinking and problem solving, communication and collaboration. These are the very skills known to prepare learners to be agile contributors on the global playing field.

Structure of a Math Workshop

To establish successful math workshops, teachers start with their intended learning outcomes, determine what work learners need to do to approach mastery of those targets, and then plan their mini-lesson by considering what kernels of insight students will need to succeed with the task at hand. The sharing and reflection component is designed as an opportunity for students not only to survey what they have accomplished, and how, but also to synthesize their thinking, learning, and next steps.

Although describing a workshop sequentially may be the clearest way to orient ourselves to the use of time, many teachers use these segments flexibly. They may sometimes start with work time or reflection, or put the mini-lesson in the middle of class. But if you are just getting started, try beginning with the classic format illustrated in figure 2.3. Then you can mix things up, as appropriate to your students and their needs, keeping your eye on the target of generating mathematical understanding.

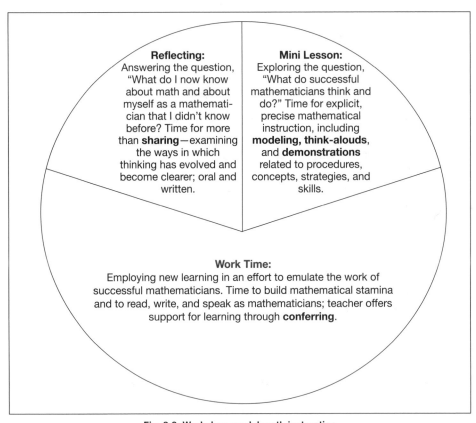

Reflecting: Answering the question, "What do I now know about math and about myself as a mathematician that I didn't know before? Time for more than **sharing**—examining the ways in which thinking has evolved and become clearer; oral and written.

Mini Lesson: Exploring the question, "What do successful mathematicians think and do?" Time for explicit, precise mathematical instruction, including **modeling, think-alouds**, and **demonstrations** related to procedures, concepts, strategies, and skills.

Work Time: Employing new learning in an effort to emulate the work of successful mathematicians. Time to build mathematical stamina and to read, write, and speak as mathematicians; teacher offers support for learning through **conferring**.

Fig. 2.3. Workshop-model math instruction

Let us look at each of those subcomponents one at a time.

Opening

Many math teachers begin class with an opening routine, whether a warm-up, problem of the day, jiffy quiz, or homework management. During a math workshop, the opening presents a key opportunity to set the stage for the class, engaging learners as thinkers and igniting their interest in the content. A predictable opening invites students to transition smoothly into the learning environment and then to use their first few minutes purposefully.

Mini-lesson

The mini-lesson is named as such because it is quick and focused. In the mini-lesson, we orient learners to the purpose of their work and apprentice them to the thinking they are about to do. A mini-lesson often includes explicit modeling through a "think aloud": The teacher narrates her own process as a problem solver, describing the invisible workings inside her own mind. In this way, a think-aloud offers learners a window into the approach of a master craftsperson managing an intellectual challenge.

A mini-lesson can include modeling of content, process skills, literacy concepts, thinking strategies, or some combination of those. It is focused on specific goals and is intended to offer le0000000000arners the skills and the understanding they need to succeed independently during the work time.

Work time

The majority of a math workshop is devoted to work time, an opportunity for learners to wrestle with interesting, challenging content both individually and in small groups. The task of the workshop needs to be thoughtful enough to engage learners' thinking in new ways, give them a lot to chew on, discuss, and decide. Rich tasks of high cognitive demand serve to invite novel approaches, open debate, summon multiple perspectives, reveal misconceptions, and sustain interest. These tasks might include multifaceted problems, projects, mathematical controversies, and more. (For a list of sources of rich math tasks, see the appendix.)

Successful learners in a math workshop know how to collaborate, sustain their stamina, and get themselves "unstuck" as needed. As teachers implementing NCTM's practices, we strive to ensure that learners' struggles are productive by offering them the support and scaffolds they need to succeed so that they can, as the Common Core describes, persevere in solving problems. These skills are learned. Thus, as facilitators, math teachers need to actively develop these skills in students. (See "Sustaining Students' Stamina" below, on page 29.)

Conferring is one key instructional strategy that teachers use during work time to promote student stamina. Conferring involves engaging individuals and small groups in purposeful conversations about their learning throughout the work time, not so much to "help" as to affirm, assess, and encourage deeper thinking and richer understanding. (Conferring will be explored further in chapter 5.)

Sharing and reflection

Although we are often tempted to leave off the final segment of a workshop, envisioning that students could "finish up their work" if we did not "stop them" just yet, experienced practitioners of workshop-model instruction know that sharing and reflection are key components of solidifying students' understanding. The closing segment of a workshop is a time for learners to gather their ideas, share them with classmates, and then look back on their own experience during the work time. Sharing can take place in pairs, small groups, or a whole-group setting, with specific prompts designed to lead learners to respond to their peers' work with more than single-syllable replies. Sentence stems and accountability scaffold these closing conversations' success.

Reflection, often saved until the very end of class, and too often skipped, is a critical chance for students to cement their learning for the day by assessing their progress toward the learning targets of the lesson, considering what they may have learned about themselves as mathematicians, and recognizing which strategies they want to tuck in their tool belts for future use. As students reflect, teachers can seize this chance to assess understanding and make plans to adjust instruction accordingly, as described by the final NCTM Mathematical Teaching Practice, "Effective teaching of mathematics uses evidence of student thinking to assess progress toward mathematical understanding and to adjust instruction continually in ways that support and extend learning" (NCTM 2014).

With a carefully crafted mini-lesson introducing critical skills and content, ample work time for student thinking and discourse, and planned sharing and reflection for inviting students' metacognition, math workshops provide an ideal forum in which teachers can experience all eight of the Common Core Standards for Mathematical Practice every day (see fig. 2.4).

Planning a Math Workshop

Many math teachers' instructional practice already approximates a workshop: We explain some concepts and let students work some problems. The growing edge for most is expanding the focus from planning what learners will be *doing* to how learners will be invited to *think as mathematicians* during that lesson. In other words, designing and facilitating a math workshop is not just about selecting activities but rather about envisioning, provoking, and scaffolding students' reasoning (individually and collectively) as mathematicians.

> **Reflect**
>
> • How do you and your students presently use math learning time? What similarities and differences do you see between what you are doing and the workshop model, as described here?

Establish the purpose: Mathematics goal

The best workshops begin with a clear understanding of the goals for learners and a strong vision on the part of the teacher of what that understanding will look like. The goal is often a standard or a benchmark or a related topic of study, but within that a teacher needs to take the time to identify specifically what he hopes students will come to understand each day.

For example, when planning a math workshop, a teacher goes beyond the topic "linear equations" and asks herself, "What is it about linear equations I am asking learners to master?" She may articulate that the focus on this particular day is the true meaning of slope, what it represents, and why. With this tight focus, she can design a task and a reflection prompt that will support students in zeroing in on their understanding of this important mathematical concept.

In addition to establishing a content learning target, we also establish one or more process targets. What is it that learners will be doing to reach this content goal? Reading? Modeling? Writing? Reasoning? Being clear about the process that will support learners in

	Teachers ...	While each student ...	Link to Common Core Standards for Mathematical Practice
Opening	• Engage learners as mathematicians	• Gets right to work on purposeful and meaningful mathematics	• Makes sense of problems and perseveres in solving them
Mini-lesson	• Set purpose • Activate background knowledge • Model thinking, content and/or process • Demonstrate use of tools • Set expectations for work time	• Engages prior knowledge • Listens, watches, takes notes • Asks clarifying questions	• Looks for and expresses regularity in repeated reasoning
Work time	• Confer with students • Support small groups as needed • Assess students' understanding	• Engages in meaningful work: problem solving, creating, discussing, reading, writing, modeling • Applies learning from mini-lesson to task • Collaborates with peers in ways that promote thinking and understanding • Documents thinking	• Makes sense of problems and perseveres in solving them • Reasons abstractly and quantitatively • Constructs viable arguments • Models with mathematics • Uses appropriate tools strategically • Attends to precision
Sharing and reflection	• Facilitate students' sharing • Connect students' learning to larger mathematical purpose of the lesson • Acknowledge students' progress and effort • Describe next steps in the learning sequence	• Shares thinking • Asks questions • Synthesizes • Monitors how understanding has grown or changed	• Critiques the reasoning of others • Looks for and makes use of structure • Looks for and expresses regularity in repeated reasoning

© PEBC, used with permission

Fig. 2.4. Math workshop integrates the Common Core Standards for Mathematical Practice.

achieving the objective will not only support their understanding but also aid us in planning a mini-lesson that includes explicit instruction, as needed, around both content and process.

Plan the task

With a clear purpose, a math workshop planner will select or design a juicy task that can focus learners' thinking on making meaning—tasks that mathematics educator Jo Boaler describes as having a "low floor and a high ceiling"—accessible to all and yet offering lots of room for growth and creativity for our most persistent learners.

A typical class exploring linear equations may devote large chunks of time to graphing equation after equation on a coordinate plane. Challenged to engage learners in deeply comprehending the meaning of slope, a workshop-model instructor may set aside her more traditional graphing activity and instead ask students to compile and compare four graphs of specific slopes, 3, –3, $1/3$, –($1/3$), and then to write an explanation of how and why those graphs differ. With this task, learners will get to the heart of the relationship that a slope describes, solidifying in their minds how to deal with m in any linear equation they may encounter. This is but one example of how tightening learning targets can impel us to refine learners' work time task; more ideas are presented in figure 2.5.

Typical topic	Typical task	Tight learning target	Students' workshop task
Pythagorean theorem	Find the hypotenuse for twenty different right triangles.	Understand the relationship between the three sides of a right triangle.	Develop a model representing why the Pythagorean theorem is true.
Combinations	Solve a series of questions about how many outfits can be created from given sets of clothes.	Understand how the number of objects in a set affects the number of possible combinations of those objects.	Develop and justify a rule for how to calculate combinations.
Factoring quadratic equations	Factor a page of equations.	Understand how and why factoring works.	Write and justify step-by-step instructions for a peer learning factoring.

Fig. 2.5. Tightening learning targets—refining tasks: examples

Often when we refine a task to make it deeper and richer, opportunities for literacy integration are apparent. Whether collaborating to discuss a concept with peers, researching mathematicians' explanations, or writing justifications of their own, learners in a math workshop rely on their reading, writing, speaking, and listening skills daily.

Design the mini-lesson: Teach content, model process

With a clear goal and a purpose-built task, a workshop designer then needs to ask herself, "What are the key skills or concepts learners will need to access this task? What are the language needs of this learning?" Here we can *resist* the temptation to model for students the very task we are about to ask them to do, thereby rescuing them from the struggle of independent thinking. Best are the mini-lessons that offer students exposure to the nature of thought required through a think-aloud about a similar, parallel problem (as modeled in the fraction lesson in "A Typical Math Workshop," pp. 17–18), without giving too much away. The goal of the workshop is to let students do the work of thinking as mathematicians, so the role of the mini-lesson is simply to foreshadow the thinking they will do, rather than explain everything. See figure 2.6 for examples of how the task planned for work time can inform the mini-lesson design.

If we want students to . . .	We might think aloud about . . .
Develop a model representing why the Pythagorean theorem is true	Modeling a different mathematical relationship, such as that between the radius and circumference of a circle
Develop and justify a rule for how to calculate combinations	Justifying a rule about a different mathematical concept, such as the distributive property
Write and justify step-by-step instructions for a peer who is learning to factor	Writing step-by-step instructions for another procedure, such as tying shoelaces, and include an explanation of why each step matters

Fig. 2.6. Developing mini-lessons to model mathematical thinking: Explaining

Scaffold work time

The rich task is the first ingredient of the work-time plan, but there is more to sort out. Workshop designers ask themselves a number of questions: Will students work independently or together? In what groupings? How will I allocate the work time, and at which points will I catch students' attention to prompt them with more information or directions? What references or resources will be available to support their stamina and independence? What will I say to groups that are "done"?

Typically workshops go best when learners launch with some independent work to get the juices of their own thoughts stewing before joining together with peers to collaborate. Solitary think time might extend just a few minutes, but this allows each learner to bring some ideas to the table when the paired or small-group conversation begins. There are many schools of thought on how to group students and how to structure group work; my suggestion is simply to change the groups often. I would always say to my middle school students on the heels of their complaints about their partners, "In real life, when you get a job, you will probably not get to decide whom you work with, so now is a good time to practice getting along with everyone."

To keep the mini-lesson short, some teachers will save a few tidbits to present to the class at some point after the group gets started on their work. In *That Workshop Book*, Samantha Bennett refers to these brief instructional interludes during work time as "catch and release": We catch learners' attention, offer input or instruction, and then release them back to independent or shared work.

For example, if students are going to be working on a task where they must create graphs, their teacher may complete a mini-lesson on reading tables and then let learners gather their materials and begin work, knowing that students will need more information later to succeed. Once he hears discussion brewing about labeling axes, he knows he can borrow students' ears for a micro-lesson on scaling graphs and using equal increments, introducing them to the decisions they will soon make about their axes and suggesting some of the questions they might want to consider. In this way, the teacher can keep the mini-lesson mini and offer learners critical information when they need it most.

Work time gives us a wonderful opportunity to sit down with learners and confer, eye to eye, and really get to know them as mathematicians. While the bulk of the class is engaged in a meaningful task, teachers are free to meet with individuals and small groups to explore their thinking, not so much to help as to provoke conversation about mathematical ideas.

Our job at this time is to listen. So the best conferring questions are those that simply get learners talking. Here are some questions to try; you might like to carry a few on your clipboard as you circulate among students:

- How's it going?

- What are you thinking?

- Can you explain/represent that in another way?

Launching conversations such as these with students during work time not only offers us windows into their thinking but also models for peers nearby how mathematicians speak to one another in ways that promote discourse. Often, once this habit is established, we will soon hear the conferring questions we ask learners repeated student to student as they hone their ability to engage with peers as thinking coaches as well.

Even the richest tasks can be completed more quickly by some students than by others. Planning ahead for this eventuality can ensure that the sweet hum of a productive workshop is not broken. So, what do learners do when they are "done"? There are many possibilities, including the following:

- Expand on their work
    - Recheck their work for accuracy
    - Justify their solution(s) with one or more explanations
    - Explore alternate strategies
    - Challenge themselves by posing and solving a similar problem
- Consult with peers
    - Share and compare processes and solutions
- Reflect on their learning
    - Write about the bigger mathematical idea (see "Reflection Prompts" on the next page)
- Practice their skills
    - Use time to complete other work or review important concepts
- Start homework

Prepare for assessment: Sharing and reflection

Identifying what constitutes evidence of understanding aids a workshop planner in knowing what he will look and listen for in that regard throughout the lesson. Planning assessment may include creating a model of a parallel product, developing a formative assessment, penning some conferring questions that can engage learners in conversations while they work, or designing a rubric for the task.

After work time, sharing and reflection present key opportunities to assess learners' progress. So, planning a workshop includes determining the format for sharing, deciding what sort of work will be shared, and selecting a reflection prompt and mode for reflection (oral, written, silent).

Reflection Prompts

- Why did we do this today?

- What is the most important thing you came to understand?

- Describe a mathematical misconception that you cleared up.

- Which strategies helped you to succeed?

- How will you help yourself remember this concept?

- When do you think you might use what you learned today?

- What do you still need to work on?

Listening in on student conversations, gathering artifacts from a day's workshop, and attending to students' comments during reflection time, the teacher gains insight into what learners have accomplished and what they need next. Then the cycle begins again: With observational data and student work in hand, we ask ourselves, "What is the next mini-lesson I need to plan to leverage learners' understanding about this content, process, or both?"

Sustaining Students' Stamina

On first learning of workshop-model instruction, some teachers balk: "My students cannot work independently for a full two-thirds of their math class!" Without preparation and practice, this may indeed be the case. The groundwork for a workshop begins with the teacher's stance and the students' dispositions, all of which can be explicitly cultivated. Workshops work best when we as teachers are committed to—

- fostering growth mindsets;
- cultivating a community of learners; and
- scaffolding student thinking.

Let's look into how.

Fostering a growth mindset

Mathematics can be difficult in general, and the work of students in a math workshop, even more so. To build the stamina required of them, learners need to cultivate growth mindsets and to understand the value of productive struggle. As Carol Dweck described in her important book *Mindset* (2006), those among us who appreciate the relationship between effort and achievement are best programmed to succeed. Drawing on her research, Dweck described a fixed mindset as a perception that intelligence is innate and unchangeable and that effort does not matter. By contrast, she characterized a growth mindset as a belief that all things are possible through determined, committed striving. Her book shares numerous examples of how individuals who adopted the latter belief, the growth mindset, overcame difficulties and achieved greatness. According to Dweck, these mindsets can be taught, and we, as teachers, are well poised to do so.

International comparative studies underline the great need to cultivate growth mindsets among U.S. students in general and U.S. math learners in particular. Researchers examining cultural differences in our perceptions of struggle found that in Asian countries, students and parents typically looked on difficulties as part and parcel of the learning process, persevering with vigor in the face of challenges. Meanwhile, American students were typically apt to give up when faced with a puzzler that appeared too difficult: We do not like to struggle, nor do we like to watch our children suffer the difficulties of working through confusion (Spiegel 2012). This aversion to struggle must be addressed to allow more students greater access to mathematical achievement, for to learn math is, indeed, to struggle.

To this end, we can each intentionally model and teach the growth mindset. We begin by explaining the differences between growth and fixed mindsets and offering learners examples of how a growth mindset has served achievers of all stripes (for ideas on this, read Dweck's book). Next, we can promote a growth mindset by noticing and naming students' stamina, praising effort rather than smartness: "Wow, Lakai, what determination you are showing as you solve this problem!" Further, we can engage learners regarding their own mindsets, guarding against deflating comments and self-denigration in the face of mistakes and instead encouraging students to adopt such phrases as "I disagree with myself" or "I am thinking about that in a new way." When we intentionally make mindset a part of our classroom conversation, we advance students' awareness of how they can craft their own success by persevering in the face of struggle.

Cultivating a community of learners

To move students out of the paradigm of inhaling bite after bite of information all week long and then spitting it back out on a Friday quiz (sometimes called "suck and puke" learning), teachers can cultivate a community of learners in which all are engaged in developing understanding through experience. This shift begins with teachers conceiving of their role as that of coach rather than of sage. As math educator Katherine Merseth told us years ago, "'Teaching as telling' can no longer be the operative form of instruction in mathematics classrooms" (Merseth 1993, p. 553). By taking the stance of learner, sitting shoulder to shoulder with students as they do the work of mathematicians, teachers communicate their confidence in their students' ability to figure things out for themselves.

Within a workshop, the teacher's stance is one of curious coach. The ideas of students are central to the workshop. Though we may prompt them by sharing the discoveries of others, ultimately learners must be invited to make sense of mathematics all by themselves. We need to trust them to do so, to bite our tongues, to allow wait time, to paraphrase rather than rescue, to turn their questions back to the group.

Believing that learners and their thinking are the heart of our workshops, we arrange our classroom environments to reflect this attitude. When possible, seating is arranged in groups or a semicircle, student work fills the walls, materials are accessible, and a document camera or other technology is available to project and share students' written work. In this way, we communicate to learners that this class is about them. To maximize students' independence during work time, consider in advance what they will need: have the rulers out, offer graph paper, point out the chart you made last week about slope. Make the classroom theirs.

Workshops are interdependent and rely on learners' ability to speak and listen to one another, to plan and collaborate, to engage in conversations about ideas, to disagree respectfully, to solve problems. Although some learners enter our classrooms prepared to be positive participants in these ways, others may need support to learn these skills. Norms can be discussed and practiced, sentence stems can seed conversation, reflection can invite students to consider how their behavior contributed to their own learning as well as to the learning of others.

A successful community of learners is founded on a belief in students and a respect for their ideas, which inform the physical layout of the classroom, the nature of the work, and the attitudes of learners. Cultivating a community of learners takes time, but this is time well spent building the life skills of responsibility for learning, collaboration, and self-sufficiency.

Scaffolding student thinking

Within the context of a workshop's juicy task, a teacher may offer students graphic organizers or other scaffolds to help them organize their work and thinking, whether solving a problem, reading a text, or planning a written piece. This book is chock-full of frameworks and models that can serve as training wheels for students as they become independent, literate mathematicians.

Scaffolds and structures that invite students to slow down, dissect a text, plan their writing, explore a vocabulary word, or discuss a solution are designed not as make-work tasks but rather as opportunities for learners to systematically experience the process of coming to understand. These activities are intended to apprentice learners in the process of making meaning for themselves. Over time, these structures, though useful, all need to be set aside so that learners can find their own way forward.

Within a workshop, teachers can model the use of structures and organizers, explain their purpose, invite learners to practice with them, and then to reflect on their utility. Some students will love three-column notes, while others will claim to be slowed down by them. Some learners will enjoy engaging in rich conversations about their ideas, while others may feel frustrated by the protocol or the time or tone of the discussion. The goal of our carefully structured instruction is not to get students to jump through the hoops of engaging in tedious tasks but rather to offer them experience with a variety of structures, activities, and tools that have the potential to make them better mathematicians.

Critical to this process is the opportunity for reflection. After offering learners new strategies to try or new experiences to explore, instructors can encourage them to ask themselves: How did this work for me? Did it help me to think clearly, to understand? Is this a strategy I would hang onto and apply in different circumstances? Ideally, after experiencing a range of tools and strategies for reading, writing, learning vocabulary, and structuring conversation, students exit our classes with a tool belt full of robust ideas they can apply independently when presented with a tough mathematical challenge at any point in the future. This is why we ask students to engage in these methodical processes: so that they can learn what it looks, feels, and sounds like to think as mathematicians.

Believe, Don't Rescue

In Denver, where I live, access to our city's swimming pools is now free for all youth, thanks to various grants and donations. Recently enjoying the warm pool on a cold day with my own children, I noticed an entire rack full of life jackets, or personal flotation devices (PFDs), as they are now known, on the pool deck. These were freely available to all "swimmers," and lifeguards were on hand to help fit the devices to any interested child or adult. I imagined that the lifeguards loved this new program, which eased their stress by ensuring that all fledgling swimmers would be prevented from sinking to the bottom of the pool. But then I began to wonder: How are these kids going to learn to swim?

The tendency to rescue children from the perils of struggle runs deep, especially among teachers. We are often the first to hand out the proverbial life vest—a hint, a correction, an answer—short-circuiting learners' opportunities to think for themselves. After all the effort we put into designing juicy tasks to engage students as thinkers, we must be vigilant to ensure that we do indeed leave the thinking and solving and discussing to the learners in our charge. As noted by the Tennessee Department of Education (2014),

> Students often struggle to solve high-level tasks. Their discomfort with the struggle when they are solving the high-level task causes them to ask the teacher for assistance. In turn, the teacher provides assistance, often by doing the problem solving for the student. The students, as a result, do not have the opportunity to learn to think, reason, and to practice engaging in problem solving and communicating.

To ensure, then, that all students have access to the challenges that will build their mathematical muscles, we teachers need to slip out of the role of lifeguard or PFD and embrace that of community coach, to spend more time asking than telling, more time observing and honoring. By not rescuing anyone from struggle, we demonstrate our belief in the innate capacity of every student. To this end, we can discipline ourselves in these ways:

- Bite our tongues, listening more than we speak.

- Sit on our hands, letting students do the writing, sketching, solving.

- Promote thinking by asking questions, identifying resources, mirroring back effective strategies.

- Notice and name, identifying and celebrating students' successes as independent problem solvers.

- Be patient, since students accustomed to spoon-feeding may not immediately cotton to the notion that their learning is in their own hands, but when we stubbornly and lovingly insist—and then support their efforts—they will learn to feed themselves.

Workshop-model instruction is a cauldron for mathematical thinking. To design and facilitate a workshop effectively, a teacher needs to know her students and the standards, envision the learning experience from the perspective of the learner, and take time to carefully plan each aspect. With an eye on promoting student thinking, we can easily see and seize opportunities to integrate the essentials of literacy—reading, writing, and speaking—as well as explicit instruction in each. Workshop-model instruction affords us a useful forum in which to hone NCTM's Mathematics Teaching Practices, address the Common Core Standards for Mathematical Practice, and integrate disciplinary literacy, all of which serve our primary purpose: growing learners' mathematical understanding.

When we believe in students and their inherent brilliance, and seize opportunities to draw that forth, the energy required to plan a workshop is a small investment that can reap tremendous gains in student achievement and self-efficacy.

"Yeah, but . . . "

- *"My students can't focus for vast swaths of work time."*

Often students come to us with little experience sustaining independent work in math, and so at the beginning of the year they may indeed not be able to work independently for any length of time. By talking with them about how to sustain their stamina, coaching them on effective problem-solving strategies, providing feedback on their strengths, and reflecting on what supported their progress, we can support all learners in progressively strengthening the muscles of their own perseverance.

- *"Kids in my classes hate working together."*

Some grown-ups hate working together, too. But collaboration is a key skill for lifelong achievement, and one that cannot be taught soon enough or practiced too much. Level with students about the sheer value of learning to work together. Troubleshoot potential rough spots in collaboration before they occur. Make their experience as a community of learners part of the ongoing reflection: What did your group members do to help one another learn today? What might you adjust tomorrow to get even more out of your time in class?

- *"We don't have time for all this!"*

Learning takes time; understanding takes even longer. Traditional curricula pressuring teachers to zoom through stacks of undigested content serve no one. The teacher ends up doing too much of the work of explaining, and the students get few opportunities to think. Rather than kidding ourselves that "covering" a chapter by doing every problem set in it achieves the standard of that chapter, we as teachers can instead begin with the learning targets and pick and choose how we spend time addressing those, winnowing down the work to those critical tasks that will ignite understanding.

 **Math Workshop Planning Template**

Reading as Mathematicians

What if we *decided* that all children—*all* children—deserve an opportunity to be approached as great thinkers? What if we chose to teach children not just the content prescribed in our curricula, but how to understand as Van Gogh understood, fervently?

—Ellin Oliver Keene, *To Understand*

Problems of the Day

- What is the relationship between reading and mathematical understanding?

- How can we support math learners in making sense of all kinds of text?

- What does reading instruction look like within a math workshop?

A friend of mine taught at a high school for recently arrived immigrants. Many of the students were of Latino descent, with families from Mexico, Guatemala, Colombia, and other Central and South American countries. When it came to P.E. class, the Spanish-speaking kids dominated the basketball court and the soccer field, leaving many of the students from Asia and Africa to watch and wish. But one day, the teacher set up some Ping-Pong tables, and all of a sudden two cousins from China crushed all their peers, hands down. This was their domain: These boys knew the equipment, the rules, the rhythm, and the strokes to dominate the game, and none of the soccer stars could touch them.

To become champions at mathematics, students must similarly find themselves at home in its context, with its numbers, texts, and syntax. Through explicit reading instruction we can support all learners in growing confident that mathematics is indeed their native land.

Why Teach Reading in Math

Historically, designers of secondary schools, authors of standards, test writers, and teachers have somehow created and perpetuated a misconception: that reading and math are entirely separate "subjects" having little to do with each other, that one ought not to have to read in math class any more than one should expect to order pizza at a sushi restaurant. But math and reading need each other. Reading is all about making sense of the world, deepening one's understanding. This purpose is central to math, too.

Math learners, as well as professionals who use math in their work, read constantly. The texts we work with can include narrative explanations and prose, yet our reading extends beyond these to include rich and varied material: diagrams, equations, graphs, charts, tables, formulas, and more. To read each of these effectively as mathematicians, learners need to be familiar with the various "genres" of mathematical writing and develop strategies for making sense of them. (These genres, samples of which appear in fig. 3.1, are discussed in more detail later in this chapter.)

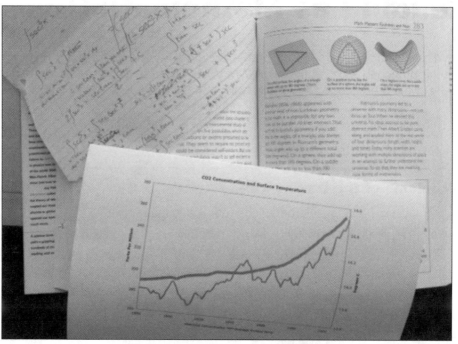

Fig. 3.1. Samples of mathematical "genres"

NCTM's Mathematics Teaching Practices invite us to "use and connect mathematical representations." To support students in doing so, we need to coach them to make meaning of all the varied representations, or texts, that they will encounter in mathematics. Comprehending a representation, whether narrative, graphic, or otherwise, requires special skills: reading skills. Reading—or making sense—is a precursor to using and connecting mathematical representations. This is why disciplinary reading is so important.

You may be thinking that your students already know how to read, and in many ways, they do. Yet, further instruction is required to support learners in tackling the unique reading demands of our discipline. Assessments alone provide strong evidence that students need additional support as readers of mathematics to be successful. Numerous researchers (Abedi and Lord 2001) note the discrepancy between learners' performance on problems in verbal and numeric formats on standardized assessments, demonstrating that students need more than mathematical skills alone to solve word problems.

Research on literacy instruction (Shanahan and Shanahan 2008) demonstrates the need for content-area teachers to engage learners in a tailored exploration of disciplinary reading. Timothy and Cynthia Shanahan describe their study along these lines: "Instead of trying to convince disciplinary teachers of the value of general reading strategies developed by reading experts, we went out to see if we could jury-rig existing ones so that they would more directly and explicitly address the specific highly specialized disciplinary reading demands of chemistry, history, and mathematics" (p. 57). In conversations with mathematics teachers, the Shanahans uncovered the numerous reading challenges of traditional math texts and explored the means to support students in deriving understanding from them.

As readers in math, learners can apply many of the same strategies they use to make sense of other texts. Yet, as the Shanahans' work points out, we as teachers also need to devote a portion of students' learning time to exploring the unique features of mathematical texts and the specialized reading skills that can support them in making sense of those. This is particularly important for English language learners, who may possess strong conceptual understanding as mathematicians but struggle simply to match up those concepts with the English words. Learning the specialized skill set required to read effectively as a mathematician enhances a learner's ability to make meaning of all nonfiction, to solve problems, and to communicate. This chapter explores the nature of mathematical texts and how we can support learners in understanding these texts deeply as a means to understanding mathematics.

What to Read?

When I was in school, math class was just one problem set after another, with little else to read. Thick math textbooks do indeed offer more than enough material for students in terms of volume, yet inviting students to enjoy a balanced diet of mathematical reading requires a bit more creativity. Without sacrificing content learning objectives, what kinds of mathematical reading material might you present? Here are some suggestions for interesting mathematical reading:

- Examples of the real-world application of the mathematical concepts you are studying

- Current events that include statistics or graphic representations

- Explanations of concepts by famous mathematicians, historical or modern

- Nonfiction texts describing mathematical phenomena

- Solutions or explanations by classroom peers

How the Common Core Literacy Standards Can Leverage Mathematical Understanding

The Common Core State Standards for Literacy in History/Social Studies, Science, and Technical Subjects: Reading (CCSSI 2010) includes an array of skills and abilities. One instructional practice highlighted as a key response to the Common Core's reading standards is "close reading." Let's give it a try. Read through the standards in figure 3.2 once to get the big idea. Then reread the standards, this time considering their relevance to your work as a math teacher: Code the text by putting a star by each that seems relevant to you and, if it serves you, feel free to cross out those that are unlikely to have a place in your math courses. (Students will be spending plenty of time in history/social studies and science to address those.)

Then, for the standards you starred, go deeper. Underline the verbs. Circle the nouns. Ask yourself, "How, specifically, might helping students master this skill also promote students' mathematical reasoning and problem solving? How might it support them as they use and connect mathematical representations? How might it help them prepare for meaningful mathematical discourse? And what might this look and sound like specifically in math class?"

After carefully reading and analyzing these literacy standards, you may also be ready for a conversation with a colleague in response. Welcome to close reading!

Key Ideas and Details

1. Read closely to determine what the text says explicitly and to make logical inferences from it; cite specific textual evidence when writing or speaking to support conclusions drawn from the text.
2. Determine central ideas or themes of a text and analyze their development; summarize the key supporting details and ideas.
3. Analyze how and why individuals, events, or ideas develop and interact over the course of a text.

Craft and Structure

4. Interpret words and phrases as they are used in a text, including determining technical, connotative, and figurative meanings, and analyze how specific word choices shape meaning or tone.
5. Analyze the structure of texts, including how specific sentences, paragraphs, and larger portions of the text (e.g., a section, chapter, scene, or stanza) relate to each other and the whole.
6. Assess how point of view or purpose shapes the content and style of a text.

Integration of Knowledge and Ideas

7. Integrate and evaluate content presented in diverse media and formats, including visually and quantitatively, as well as in words.
8. Delineate and evaluate the argument and specific claims in a text, including the validity of the reasoning as well as the relevance and sufficiency of the evidence.
9. Analyze how two or more texts address similar themes or topics to build knowledge or to compare the approaches the authors take.

Range of Reading and Level of Text Complexity

10. Read and comprehend complex literary and informational texts independently and proficiently.

Fig. 3.2. Common Core State Standards: College and Career Readiness Anchor Standards for Reading (CCSSI 2010)

What did you find? Which standards seem relevant and useful to learners in service of their mathematical mastery? Which could possibly connect to your work in math class? Which seem tangential to your instructional purpose? Which are irrelevant?

In "Teaching Disciplinary Literacy to Adolescents: Rethinking Content-Area Literacy," literacy experts Timothy and Cynthia Shanahan (2008) write that reading mathematics requires—

- intensive consideration of text, word by word;

- rereading;

- emphasis on error-detection; and

- precision of understanding.

Almost all mathematical text is, in effect, what the Common Core would call "complex" text: dense with abstract concepts, convoluted syntax, and challenging vocabulary (for more on vocabulary, see chapter 4).

We can support learners in growing the mathematical reading habits that the Shanahans describe by providing students with explicit reading instruction integrated on a regular basis into our courses. This, in turn, will cultivate students' independence as mathematical thinkers and problem solvers.

How Do Readers Make Sense?

Think of yourself as a reader. When perusing *People* magazine at the dentist's office, you probably have an easy time understanding the text and images, so you don't need to rely on any specific, notable reading strategies. But when confronted with the opportunity to select between cell phone plans with different initiation costs; device discounts; fee structures for talk minutes, text messaging, and data; contract lengths; service areas; and so forth, you may find yourself needing to wrestle a bit to make sense of it all. What strategies do you employ? Some folks may find themselves marking up the brochures, others may start making lists or tables, and some may want to consult with a friend, while a few customers may go straight to a graphing calculator. There are many ways to make sense of different cell phone plans, just as there are a lot of ways to make sense of mathematical texts.

What do you notice yourself doing to make meaning of complex text as a mathematician? As a successful adult, you have a collection of strategies, either conscious or unconscious, for unraveling complex texts or circumstances. You might find that you draw on these with such automaticity that you do not even realize you are doing so. Some young mathematicians come by comprehension and problem-solving strategies naturally, but many do not.

When we explicitly teach math students the means to make sense of challenging text and invite them to practice and reflect on those strategies, we offer them skills for lifelong learning. Effective disciplinary literacy instruction starts with us noticing what we ourselves do to make sense of mathematical representations and writing, and then developing a plan to convey those same useful approaches to students, as well as to invite their metacognition (self-awareness) about their own strategies.

Surface and Deep Structure

Linguist Noam Chomsky (1957) describes two layers that readers need to navigate to make sense: surface structures (which involve syntax and how a text "looks" and "sounds") and deep structures (which relate to what a text means). In mathematics, surface structure could be described as the way things are being said—the text features, genre, style, order of a piece—while deep structures refer to the underlying idea or concept intended to be communicated.

For example, "2 × 2 = 4," on the surface, appears to a reader to be very different from the statement "two twos are four," yet on a deep level, their meaning is the same. To succeed as readers in all contexts, one must navigate both surface and deep structure.

Surface Structures in Mathematical Text

To access mathematics texts at the surface level, learners need to be familiar with mathematical syntax, text features, and the genres of mathematics. Much of the following description of surface structures may appear exceedingly obvious to you, a skilled and experienced mathematician, yet learners may not gain this knowledge by osmosis and will benefit from explicit instruction on decoding the surface structures of mathematical writings.

Syntax

If you are old enough to have learned to program on an Apple II computer, you are probably familiar with the term *Syntax Error*, which often popped up on the screen at me and my friends when we tried to get our 128K machine to do such things as type our names in inverse characters and flash them at us eternally. We learned that to get the computer to do what we wanted it to do, we had to talk to it in a very specific way, using the proper syntax of the programming language. Still today, for users of calculators, applets, and other tools, syntax—the way we say things—matters. Consider these expressions:

$$5 \times 2 \qquad 5 * 2 \qquad 5 \cdot 2 \qquad 5(2)$$

Each represents the exact same operation, yet a reader without a grasp of the syntax of mathematics may find herself completely flummoxed when asked to compare them. To make sense of mathematics as readers, students need to comprehend the meaning of mathematical syntax, of symbolic representations. To scaffold students' mathematical understanding, teachers can devote time to explicit instruction of individual symbols and what they represent, as well as to describing their meaning in combination with others.

Text features

Did you just read those words: *text features*? Did you start in that moment wondering what those might be and how they could be of any use to you as a math teacher? If yes, great! Those words were a cue for you, highlighting the big idea of this section.

It might surprise you that students often skip over titles and headings like that, and dive directly into the prose in front of them. As adult readers, we may take for granted how text structures support us in accessing the content. We know what a title represents, what captions are for, and when we can safely skim and scan for important content. Some students naturally grow their own understanding of these text structures and leverage them to support their comprehension; still others tend to undermine their own understanding by ignoring these intentional supports.

Authors and editors go to great lengths to format texts in ways that orient a reader to the main ideas and important details, yet too often naïve readers miss these clues. We can

Teaching Text Features

Eighth-grade teacher Chad Griffiths projects a graph onto the interactive whiteboard as his students enter class. These instructions appear in a yellow box on the side: "In your math notebooks, write down three things you know about this graph."

Students write silently for a few minutes. Then Mr. Griffiths calls on Alex to share. Alex says, "It's about temperature over time."

"How do you know?"

"The title, it says 'Average Temperature at the North Pole,' and across the bottom, it has the different months of the year listed."

Mr. Griffiths thanks Alex and asks her to come up and point to that title, and then he engages the class in a discussion about where one typically finds the title of a graph—on the top, across the bottom, sometimes down one side, usually in a large font, they agree—and he records their observations on a piece of chart paper.

Next, Chance shares, "It's in Celsius."

"How do you know?"

"There, on the y-axis, it says 'Temperature,' and in parenthesis, 'Degrees Celsius.'" As Chance is talking, Mr. Griffiths waves him to the front, and the student points out the label on the y-axis as he finishes his sentence.

"So, that axis is labeled with the thing being measured, temperature, and then the units of measure in parenthesis," Mr. Griffiths affirms and jots notes on the chart paper about labels. "Could the temperature be measured in a different unit?" he asks the class.

"Fahrenheit!" and "Kelvin!" students offer.

"So it's a good thing they told us here, 'Celsius,' so we know what we are measuring in."

In just a few minutes, Mr. Griffiths has reminded some students and informed others about the key text features one needs to seek out to understand a graph. With brief, regular, intentional conversations like this about text features in a variety of genres, he scaffolds students' ability to make sense as mathematicians.

support students' strategic reading of mathematics by taking the time to explain, model, and discuss how to take advantage of text features. Here are some to attend to:

- Captions
- Glossary
- Graphics

- Illustrations
- Index
- Subtitles
- Special print (boldface, italics)
- Textboxes

Studying the specific genres of mathematical text

In addition to text features, some of which can be found across content areas, math readers also need to understand the specific genres—writing styles—used to convey mathematical ideas.

Throughout their years in language arts classes, students will read and devote time to analyzing a variety of genres: biography, poetry, play, novel, and so forth. Similarly, we can support learners in making sense of mathematics by explicitly introducing and discussing, one at a time, the many genres that math learners read: expository prose, word problems, graphic representations, formulas and equations, solutions and proofs, rubrics, and more. Each has its unique format and structure, which, when understood, can significantly support the reader's comprehension.

Given that you are a mathematical native, analysis of these genres may seem too elementary or obvious to you. Yet a surprising number of students find simple conversations along these lines illuminating. Let us take a moment to step back and analyze some of the typical genres of math learning shown in figure 3.3, so that we, in turn, can offer students explicit explanations of how, as readers, they can make sense of each.

Genre	Purpose	Typical text features	Reading tips
Expository writing	Explains mathematical phenomena	• Title • Boldfaced or italicized words • Definitions • Diagrams or illustrations	• Note the title, and set a purpose as a reader. • Ensure comprehension of key concepts and terms. • Study diagrams closely and make connections to narrative text.
Word problem	Poses a problem to solve mathematically	• Puts mathematics into a context • Usually includes data needed • Problem to solve usually comes at the end of text	• Home in on the question you need to answer and then reread for helpful information. • Pay careful attention to units of measure.
Graphic representation	Organizes data	• Title • Labels • Units of measure	• Use text features to get oriented. • Check for scale to ensure understanding of patterns. • Notice high points, low points, trends, and outliers. • Strive to synthesize into a message.

Fig. 3.3. Genres of mathematical text

Genre	Purpose	Typical text features	Reading tips
Formulas and equations	Describes relationships	• Includes letters, numbers, and symbols • May be supported with illustrations or diagrams	• Strive to understand the big idea behind the equation: What is the relationship being described? • Grasp when and how this equation is useful. • Know what each symbol represents. • Identify variables and constants.
Solution and proof	Explains how a result was derived	• Demonstrates steps in a process • May include calculations and visuals • May refer to principles or theorems as justification	• Know the author's purpose. • Strive to understand the logic as you read step by step. • Ask yourself whether the strategy is appropriate, whether the steps are accurate, and whether the solution makes sense.
Rubric	Offers description of high-quality work	• Describes expectations • Details how a learner can demonstrate proficiency • Identifies what the assessor values	• Look for the big picture: What are you being asked to do? How will you be assessed? • Familiarize yourself with the rows or categories of the assessment. • Ensure that you understand the terms and expectations before beginning the project. • Realistically evaluate your own work according to the rubric before submitting.

Fig. 3.3. *Continued*

Even a few minutes devoted to analyzing a genre, highlighting a text feature, or examining a syntax situation can enhance learners' access to mathematical texts. Do your students really need this kind of teaching? They probably experienced a lot of this type of instruction in surface structures in elementary school with general subject texts, but as they enter middle and high school and face new content-area reading demands, explicit mathematics-specific surface structure reading instruction can greatly support readers of all stripes.

Deep Structure in Mathematical Text

The surface structures discussed above include those aspects of a text that allow a reader to "get" what it is saying at a basic level. By contrast, deep structures involve conveying the richer meaning behind the words or formulas. Some authors explain the relationship between these with an analogy of an iceberg: The surface structure represents what can be seen above water, and the deep structure refers to all the underlying meaning and richness supporting that idea.

For example, take the oft-stated $a^2 + b^2 = c^2$. On a surface level, this can be read as an equation with a couple of variables, each raised to a power of 2, which add up to another variable raised to the same power. That is indeed what it says, on a surface level. Yet, to understand this equation on a deeper level, a reader needs to grasp that the variables represent the side lengths of a right triangle and that the equation describes a mathematical relationship attributed to Pythagoras of Greece, more than 2500 years ago—and furthermore, that this relationship can be proved by a variety of mathematical means, an understanding of which would represent a deep grasp the notion $a^2 + b^2 = c^2$.

Therefore, to take students beyond a superficial reading of mathematics and to support them in building understanding as mathematicians, we need to offer specific strategies for going below the surface to uncover the depths of the mathematical ideas and problems they read.

Thinking strategies for mathematicians

A few decades ago, David Pearson and colleagues (1992) investigated the sorts of behaviors that proficient readers across all content areas engage in as they strive to make sense of text. Over and over again, respondents to their inquiry reported applying a distinct set of strategies when faced with the challenge of coming to understand complex texts. Pearson and his colleagues found that proficient readers—

- ask questions;
- determine importance;
- draw on background knowledge;
- infer;
- visualize;
- monitor for meaning; and
- synthesize.

Armed with this list of strategies, some early literacy teachers, in turn, sought to instruct beginning readers about these tools for making sense of text, and with great results. Thus emerged the work of thinking strategy instruction, work that teachers now find useful and relevant at all grade levels and across the curriculum. The purpose of thinking strategy instruction is to offer learners approaches that they can internalize and apply flexibly to understand information deeply.

Mathematicians can use these thinking strategies for a variety of purposes: reading, problem solving, and critiquing the work of others, before, during, and after engaging in that work. Figure 3.4 orients us to some of the ways in which readers of mathematical texts can apply each strategy.

44

Thinking strategy	As readers of content... *As mathematicians read reference books, textbooks, and other resources to gather information and understand mathematical ideas, they . . .*	As problem solvers . . . *Mathematicians study problems to solve them. As problem solvers, mathematicians . . .*	Sounds like . . .
Ask questions	• Ponder whether concepts make sense • Wonder how new ideas connect with prior knowledge • Consider areas of confusion • Wonder how to use new information	• Wonder about the nature of the problem • Wonder about the purpose of the problem • Ask for information • Wonder which strategy to use to solve • Wonder what pitfalls to watch for in the problem-solving process	• Does this make sense? • What am I supposed to find out? • What do I already know? • What else do I need?
Determine importance	• Set a purpose for their reading • Search for the main ideas • Identify important examples that help them understand • Find special conditions or common misconceptions	• Identify what the problem is asking • Select relevant data • Identify potential pitfalls in the problem-solving process • Consider special criteria that may be unique to each problem • Assess whether their answer makes sense	• So, what I need to know is . . . • This is important because . . . • I can use this by . . . • This is an example of the big idea . . .
Draw on background knowledge	• Build new background knowledge as needed • Pay attention to when they have background knowledge about a concept, and to how their background knowledge helps them to understand • Assess the accuracy of their background knowledge • Build, revise, or delete background knowledge as needed • Make connections between new ideas and concepts they already know	• Make meaning of key vocabulary • Understand the type of mathematics they are being asked to do • Develop problem-solving plans to suit the situation • Use what they know about related problems to solve new problems efficiently and accurately	• What I already know about this is . . . • Oh, this reminds me of . . . • This connects with my background knowledge . . . • I disagree with myself: I used to think . . . but now I think . . .

Fig. 3.4. Thinking strategies for mathematicians

Thinking strategy	As readers of content... *As mathematicians read reference books, textbooks, and other resources to gather information and under-stand mathematical ideas, they . . .*	As problem solvers . . . *Mathematicians study problems to solve them. As problem solvers, mathematicians . . .*	Sounds like . . .
Infer	• Draw conclusions not explicitly stated in the text	• Make decisions about how to approach problems • Analyze data to identify patterns • Make predictions based on information given	• So, what we are being asked to figure out is . . . • I predict . . . • What we need to do is . . . • The pattern is . . .
Make mental models (adapted for mathematics from "Visualize")	• Pause to represent information and ideas in graphs, charts, draw-ings, diagrams, etc. • Create symbolic representations that help them to remember information	• Organize what they know about a problem • Represent abstract re-lationships concretely • Develop a system for solving a problem • Represent their thinking and solution	• I can represent this by . . . • Another way to show this is . . .
Monitor for meaning	• Maintain awareness of when they do and do not understand • Notice confusion and stop to address it	• Ensure that they un-derstand the context and situation before beginning to solve a problem • Stop to classify the type of work the problem is asking them to do	• The part I do under-stand is . . . • I am confused about . . . • My question is . . .
Synthesize	• Draw together various pieces of information from disparate sources • Integrate new infor-mation to grow their understanding of concepts • Notice their thinking changing over time	• Generalize from patterns • Match a strategy to a problem • Apply concepts in new contexts • Develop solutions that integrate more than one mathematical strand	• This is an example of . . . • The relationship between . . . and . . . is . . . because . . . • The pattern is . . . • One strategy that might help is . . . • What I already know about . . . can help me . . .

Fig. 3.4. *Continued*

Thinking Strategy Instruction in a Math Workshop

Of the seven thinking strategies uncovered by Pearson and colleagues (1992) and shown in figure 3.4, which do you find yourself using most often to make meaning of a text? Which make the most sense to you as a mathematician?

Hark back to chapter 2 and our discussion of apprenticing students as mathematicians through a math workshop. Effective thinking strategy instruction follows the familiar pattern of the workshop model: describe the strategies, model their use, invite learners to rehearse them explicitly in the context of their content learning, and then ask them to be self-aware about a particular strategy's efficacy: How did this help you to understand?

Though there are seven distinct thinking strategies named in figure 3.4, we need not teach all of them in the context of math learning, nor do we need to teach them in any particular order. As you play around with them, you will find that they bleed into one another, yet are distinct. Still, students are best served when we discuss the strategies one at a time, devoting attention to exploring their unique nuance and functionality. Often math teachers will pair one strategy with a specific math unit of instruction and spend time exploring how that strategy serves learners' understanding while focusing on the content learning objective across time.

Metacognition is thinking about your own thinking, noticing what mental moves you make to arrive at meaning. Give it a go: Read the following passage for understanding and, as you do so, pay attention to how your mind works to make sense. What strategies come naturally to you? How might you explain your approach to students? (This is fodder for your mini-lesson.)

Eratosthenes (276–195 BCE) calculated the circumference of the earth by comparing the angles of the sun's rays entering deep wells at two separate locations in Egypt on the summer solstice. In Syene, at noon that day, the sun was directly overhead (a zenith distance of 0°), while in Alexandria (latitude 23.5°), the sun's zenith distance was 7°. He used angle measurements, the known distance between the cities (800 km), geometry, and ratios to estimate the circumference of the earth.

Mini-lesson

A mini-lesson within a workshop is an ideal time to introduce, explain, model, or reinforce a thinking strategy.

Introducing the strategy

When we first present thinking strategies to learners, they are comforted to know that this is not a new exercise we are asking them to do just for the sake of our academic content area but rather a familiar approach they may already be using in their lives. Introducing a strategy need not take a long time but can be effective when we describe the strategy in general, tell stories about the strategy in our own life experience (not necessarily in math), and invite learners to do the same. Students' awareness of the strategy can also be facilitated by creating and presenting an anchor chart—a poster-sized, one-frame cartoon—representing and reminding them of the strategy's meaning.

Let's listen in as Ms. X introduces the strategy of determining importance to her class:

> "So, this weekend, we were going to a movie, and just as we were about to leave the kids with the babysitter, my two-year-old son had a total meltdown and was begging me for some chocolate milk. We don't buy chocolate milk, but we buy milk and Hershey's syrup, so I am there thinking to myself, 'If I take the time to mix that all together before I go, I am going to be late to the movie,' but then I looked down at his freaked-out little face and looked over at the babysitter's nervousness and decided it was better to leave them on a strong footing than to rush out and catch the previews. I made the chocolate milk because right then, making that for him was the most important thing to do.

> "Think about a time in your own life when you had to determine importance," she invites. "Then go ahead and turn and talk to your neighbor about that." Students pair and share stories and then come together as a class to offer a few examples: the time my favorite jeans were in the dryer, but I wanted to wear them anyway so put them on wet; the time I really wanted breakfast but knew that stopping to eat would make me late for my soccer game; the time I stayed out late skateboarding, even though I knew I would get into trouble with my parents.

> After this brief sharing, Ms. X shares an anchor chart she had quickly created (see fig. 3.5). On the right is a horse; on the left, Betsy Ross stitching an American flag; and in the middle, a pile of hay with a needle in it. "What's important?" she asks the group.

> "If you are the horse, the hay is most important," one student volunteers.

> "And if you are Betsy Ross," another chimes in, "you probably care about the needle."

> "Exactly," Ms. X affirms. "So what is important depends on who you are and what you are trying to accomplish."

Fig. 3.5. "Determining importance" anchor chart

Modeling

Once we have connected learners with the strategy by exploring its utility in daily life, we can prepare them to apply it to their academic work. Explain that this strategy is not just a gymnastics move we want to rehearse in this unit but rather a lifelong learning skill they can pack into the hard drive of their minds and reapply at their leisure throughout their learning careers. Still, for practice's sake, we can explain, we are going to try it out with some math.

To model, choose any text—an introduction of a concept from the book, a word problem, a table—project that on the screen up front, and then simply think out loud about how you make sense of that text by employing the strategy at hand. Let's go back to Ms. X and hear how she determines importance:

> Ms. X starts with a word problem projected under the document camera:
>
>> The City of Napa, population 77,876, wants to build a patio surrounding a rectangular 12-by-20-meter reflecting pool in a park. They would like the patio to be 3.5 meters wide. They are deciding whether to use flagstone, which costs $29.50 per square meter, or concrete, which costs $11.75 for the same. Calculate the cost of the patio for each of these surface materials.
>
> Modeling close reading, Ms. X reads the text aloud once to get the gist and then shares her thinking: "So, I am trying to sort out what is really important here. In social studies or science textbooks, the important information is often contained in the first sentence of a paragraph, the topic sentence. But in math, we usually find the big idea at the end. Let's see . . ." She rereads the final sentence of the word problem: "Calculate the cost of the patio," and underlines it (see fig. 3.6). "That is my purpose. So, if that is my purpose, then what is important?" She starts back at the beginning of the problem and reads again, "'Population 77,876.' Is that important if I am trying to find the cost of the patio?" she asks the group.
>
> "No," they agree. She crosses it out.

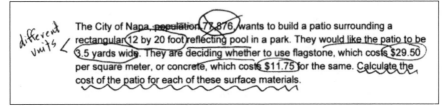

Fig. 3.6. Ms. X's sorting of unimportant and important items

> She reads on: "'A 12-by-20-meter reflecting pool.' Is that important?"
>
> Students call out. Some say yes, some say no. "Why or why not?" she invites.
>
> "You have to use that to know the surface area of the patio," explains Paulo. Peers agree.
>
> "Okay, let me start writing this down," says Ms. X, and places a graphic organizer (see fig. 3.7) under the document camera.

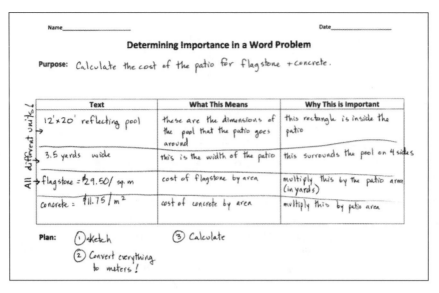

Fig. 3.7. Ms. X's use of a graphic organizer

Work Time

After modeling a thinking strategy, we need to offer learners an opportunity to try it themselves on a juicy math challenge with the support of a structure to hold their thinking. During work time, we can be explicit about both content—solving the problems—and process—using the strategy intentionally.

Students are most likely to need and apply strategies when their work causes a struggle and requires them to stretch the muscles of their minds. So, if we want to invite learners to apply thinking strategies, the tasks we offer them during work time must go beyond typical worksheet problems and instead offer complexity, ambiguity, and opportunities to synthesize various strands of mathematics. Many wonderful, Common Core–aligned sources for interesting math problems are available online, align well with our curricula, and offer learners rich problem-solving experiences. (See the appendix for problem source ideas.)

Let's see what Ms. X does next:

Having demonstrated how she uses determining importance to help her make meaning of a word problem, Ms. X offers each of her students a blank copy of the graphic organizer and a selection of five similar applied geometry problems at various levels of challenge. She invites them to choose two or three of the problems to solve while using this strategy and organizer.

"Now, some of you are going to be thinking, 'Why should I slow down and write all this out on here when I already know how to do this problem?' and I can relate to that feeling, wanting to get done. But today is not about rushing through; it's about taking the time to understand what you are reading, to think through your solution. This is how you can practice strategies that will then be transferrable to other contexts in your future."

As students work, Ms. X takes time to visit and confer with individuals and small groups about their thinking and their implementation of the strategy. She asks a variety of questions:

• How are you determining importance?

• How is that helping you to make sense?

• What is different for you because you are working with this strategy?

She pauses long enough in conversations to learn of students' victories, coach them through challenges, and address concerns. When learners need help, they know to rely on their peers, resources in the classroom, and their materials before interrupting their teacher's conferring conversations.

Holding Thinking

One great way to engage readers as thinkers is to offer them a way to respond to the text, to hold their own thinking as they read. This can take a variety of forms, including—

- coding with symbols (underlines, stars, question marks, and so forth; see Ms. X's markings in the City of Napa patio problem);

- annotating the text with margin notes;

- marking the text with sticky notes;

- recording information and ideas in a graphic organizer; and

- free writing, sketching, or drawing.

Students engage most successfully with these strategies when we explain and model them, ask learners to try them out, and then reflect on how the process of holding thinking supported their understanding.

Sharing and reflection

Time to share and reflect is a critical component of any workshop. When working with a thinking strategy, this closing segment can revisit not only the content students explored but also the efficacy of the strategy they were striving to apply. Sharing can be a very efficient process. Rather than listening silently as a group while a single student recites his solutions to a problem, learners speak individually with a partner or a small group of folks outside their problem-solving team. Let's see how Ms. X wraps up her lesson:

As work time winds down, Ms. X asks all students to find a stopping place and to prepare to share. She then designates one area of the room for each of the five problems that students could have chosen to solve and asks learners to head to the area representing the question they are most interested in discussing. Students make decisions and scatter around the room, papers in hand. Next, she projects a slide with directions:

• Share your solution and how you arrived there. Discuss what your work has in common and how it is different.

• Talk about your experience as a problem solver using the thinking strategy "determining importance."

She reads these directions aloud and then asks students to pair with a partner or form a trio for conversations among the students in the same area of the room. Familiar with Ms. X's routine of "warm calling" on them after they have had time to talk in small groups, all students get right into their discussions. ("Warm calling" is discussed in more detail in chapter 4.) After a few minutes, Ms. X calls them back together to revisit those two questions as a whole group, calling on students randomly with an invitation to share what their partner has said.

More Resources on Content-Area Reading

Mosaic of Thought: The Power of Comprehension Strategy Instruction, by Ellin Oliver Keene and Susan Zimmermann

Do I Really Have to Teach Reading? by Cris Tovani

Strategies That Work: Teaching Comprehension to Enhance Understanding, by Stephanie Harvey and Anne Goudvis

Subjects Matter: Every Teacher's Guide to Content Area Reading, by Harvey Daniels and Steven Zemelman

---

Scaffolding Readers' Independence

"Any teacher is the best reader of the content they are teaching. If you are able to slow your thinking down a little and notice things that you do when you read content materials, you can teach the strategies you use to students," explains teacher and literacy consultant Cris Tovani (2004, p. 35). We, as math teachers and math "natives," are the adults in the best positions in our school to teach students the specialized disciplinary literacy of reading mathematical texts.

We have looked at a few specific examples of how teachers scaffolded learners' understanding of surface and deep text structures with explicit reading instruction. The confines of this book do not allow for additional examples illuminating each aspect of reading instruction. But take heart: Regardless of the text, the principles are same:

- Take time to be explicit about syntax, genres, and text features.

- Introduce learners to a balanced diet of mathematical reading.

- Make the invisible process of coming to understand visible by modeling your thinking, as well as inviting students to share theirs.

- Invite learners to explicitly practice applying thinking strategies in structured ways.

- Create time for students to reflect on how surface structure knowledge or thinking strategies help them to succeed.

By devoting energy and effort to conscious conversations about reading as mathematicians, you will support all learners in honing their abilities to make sense of mathematical texts for themselves. When students can draw meaning from a text, they are poised to engage as mathematicians with all the Common Core Standards for Mathematical Practice. Yet they must begin, as those Common Core authors noted, with practice 1: "Make sense of problems and persevere in solving them" (CCSSI 2010). Instruction in reading as mathematicians, therefore, must be the starting point of all our efforts to cultivate learners' mathematical understanding.

"Yeah, but . . . "

- *"Kids get irritated when I ask them to read in math."*

Well, now is a good time to support them in getting over that, because as they move onward in their education, take standardized assessments, and pursue any higher math, more and more reading will be required! By modeling enthusiasm for reading in mathematics, explaining the importance of developing content-area reading strategies, and offering students opportunities to practice reading as mathematicians, we cultivate their appreciation for the role of literacy in mathematics.

- *"My students already learned thinking strategies in their language arts classes."*

Wonderful! If students are already familiar with the strategies, you can really propel their mathematical understanding by explicitly taking the time to model, practice, and discuss the application of those strategies with math texts. This will be somewhat different from how they used the strategies in language arts, so you are wise to continue to devote time to modeling and practicing thinking strategies in authentic contexts within your students' math learning time.

- *"No one likes to slow down, annotate text, fill in graphic organizers. It takes too much time."*

When the work is straightforward, students don't need scaffolds or systems to organize their ideas, and these structures can feel tedious. Once the challenge gets steeper, learners do benefit from slowing down, holding their thinking, and taking time to ponder the meaning of a text. This can be frustrating to youth languishing under the impression that school is a race. Remind them that learning is about thinking, and thinking takes time.

- *"When they get to the SAT, they will not have graphic organizers, so aren't these crutches slowing them down?"*

Before students have to perform solo on standardized assessments, we can train them in the habits of mind they will need to succeed. Graphic organizers are one useful tool in this regard, scaffolding learners' thinking. Over time, we can remove the support of graphic organizers and invite students to develop their own means of organizing data as problem solvers.

- **Problem-Solving Scaffold**
- **Math Workshop Planning Template: Teaching a Thinking Strategy for Math Reading**

Developing Vocabulary for Mathematical Understanding

Everyone has experienced how learning an appropriate name for what was dim and vague cleared up and crystallized the whole matter. Some meaning seems distinct almost within reach, but is elusive; it refuses to condense into definite form; the attaching of a word somehow (just how, it is almost impossible to say) puts limits around the meaning, draws it out from the void, makes it stand out as an entity on its own account."

—John Dewey, *How We Think*

Problems of the Day

- How can vocabulary instruction support mathematical understanding?
- Given limited instructional time, which words are worth studying?
- How does effective vocabulary instruction look and sound?

Let's listen in as eighth graders, mostly English language learners, in Deb Maruyama's class hone their mathematical vocabularies while discussing the term *exponential form*. They begin by exploring the concept of an exponent's base.

Magdalena:	When I think of *base*, I think of the beginning of something.
Ms. Maruyama:	Because . . . ?
Magdalena:	Because—like a flower—the bottom is the base.
Ms. Maruyama:	[*Asking the class*] Are you understanding? What did she connect to?
Solomon:	Base and flower.
Ms. Maruyama:	Where is that coming from?
Tomas:	Her background knowledge.

Cassidy: The base is the support.

Ms. Maruyama: What makes you think that?

Charlie: I'm using Maddie's example again—the base can stand alone. The 2 can just stay there. It doesn't have to have another number with it.

[*A student whispers, clarifying her thinking to her shoulder partner, and her shoulder partner whispers back, "You should say that."*]

Ms. Maruyama: What did they do to figure that out?

Gus: They connected to the highlighted words and used their background knowledge.

Jane: They noticed the important words.

Ms. Maruyama: How?

Marguerite: They looked at the words that they already knew, which were *exponent*, *base*, *standard*, and used those to figure out the rest of the text.

Amelia: They looked for words that jumped out because they were highlighted, and then looked for words they recognized and had background knowledge about. And then looked at the surrounding words. For example, for *exponent*, the sentence before it.

Ms. Maruyama: When you're trying to figure out the meaning, can you see that they made connections to other words physically close to those words. You'll find that close to the "pop-out" words are other words that will give you clues to definitions. So, write down a definition of *exponential form*. Talk for 30 seconds.

Matthew: *Exponential form* is a number to a power.

Noe: It's when you have a string of factors in standard form and you grab the number of factors, that's the base, and you need it to build exponential form.

[*A student is at the board recording her peers' comments during this sharing.*]

Latrice: To add on to Noe's thinking, exponential form is when you have a multiplication problem, and you write it a simpler way.

Ms. Maruyama: Raise your hand if you have brother or sister less than one year old. [*Calls on those students with hands raised.*]

Selena: Exponential form is when you want to break down a multiplication problem that has the same factor.

Lisa: It's a quantity expressed by a number.

Ms. Maruyama: Do not read from the book.

Jaime: It's a string of factors—the number that's being multiplied more than once—it's a string of the same factor being multiplied more than once.

Ms. Maruyama: You're almost there. You're saying that it's $2 \times 2 \times 2 \times 2 \times 2$?

Gus: That factor that's being used more than once is the base.

[*A peer is whispering to him, "Say, 'It's a simpler form . . .'"*]

Gus: Exponential form is a simpler form to write a long string of products that have the same factor being multiplied more than once.

Ms. Maruyama: So we've incorporated Noe's, Selena's, Jamie's, Gus's [ideas]. Who can help?

Jesus: Exponential form is the shortcut to writing a long string of the same factor multiplied more than once.

Ms. Maruyama: Do you want to say "shortcut" or "simpler way"? Okay, here's my exponential form: z29%$#@. That's the simpler way to write this whole paragraph.

Tomas: We need to describe that it's a simpler form.

Solomon: [*Repeats what's written on the board, and then adds to it*] The factor being used more than once is the base, and how many times the factor's being multiplied is the exponent.

Ms. Maruyama: Nice job. I know that this took a long time. But you'll get better at this. Nice job thinking. Outstanding.

1,025,109.8

According to the Global Language Monitor, the number 1,025,109.8 represents how many words were in the English language as of January 1, 2014. (Now, I am not sure how a language can include four-fifths of a word, but let's leave that aside for now.) Consider the vastness of this number, and then the number of words you yourself may know as a fraction of those more than one million words. Then, consider the growth rate of our language: A new word is created every ninety minutes, adding nearly fifteen words a day to the English lexicon. Word learning, therefore, is a critical part of life as an English speaker.

Students come to us with various levels of vocabulary development and a variety of experiences in learning new words. In fact, according to Beck, McKeown, and Kucan (2002), high-knowledge third graders have vocabularies about equivalent to our lowest-performing high school seniors. How can this be? Researchers Hart and Risley (1995) estimate that by age 3, less advantaged students have heard thirty million fewer words than their more advantaged peers; the same authors estimate those less advantaged students' vocabularies to be half the size of their more advantaged counterparts'. On entering preschool, therefore, some students are already lagging in their vocabulary development.

To catch up is difficult: A synthesis of the research on vocabulary acquisition tells us that a typical student learns roughly 3,000 words per school year. Suppose that students with average vocabularies come to school knowing 6,000 words, while their less advantaged contemporaries know 3,000. One year later, that first group of students' total vocabularies has grown to 9,000 words (6,000 + 3,000), or a growth rate of $y = 3000x + 6,000$. Without intervention, students entering school with smaller vocabularies continue to lag behind, gaining new words at a rate half that of their peers: year one of school, 3,000 + 1,500 = 4,500 words, and their vocabulary growth rate would be described by the equation $y = 1,500x + 3,000$. If we graph those two lines, we see that they will never intersect (see fig. 4.1).

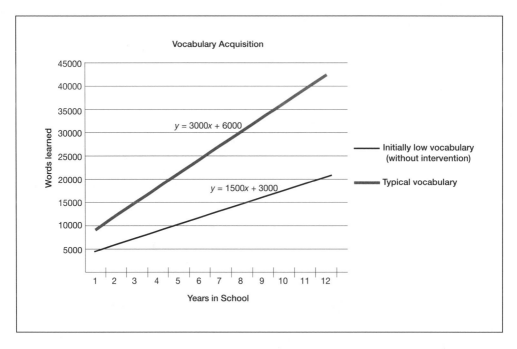

Fig. 4.1. Vocabulary acquisition graph

Without intervention, those students who began school with smaller vocabularies will continue to lag behind; by the time they reach middle and high school, this deficit poses a significant risk factor for school achievement and high school graduation. Slow vocabulary development puts English language learners, in particular, at risk. Without the necessary academic language development opportunities, these students struggle to comprehend text at their grade level, and they are also at a higher risk of being misdiagnosed as learning disabled (August et al. 2005).

Radical intervention is required to change the historical disparity in word learning and put the low-vocabulary students on an exponential learning curve. As Beck, McKeown, and Kucan (2002) write, "A large vocabulary repertoire facilitates becoming an educated person to the extent that vocabulary knowledge is strongly related to reading proficiency in particular and school achievement in general" (p. 1). Even in mathematics, academic vocabulary development facilitates understanding. The research behind the Common Core State Standards indicates that vocabulary development is one of the highest-leverage moves for increasing students' reading comprehension and word knowledge; for this reason, these new standards devote explicit attention to vocabulary:

> Common Core State Standards: College and Career Readiness Anchor Standards for Language (specifically Vocabulary Acquisition and Use)

> L.4. Determine or clarify the meaning of unknown and multiple-meaning words and phrases by using context clues, analyzing meaningful word parts, and consulting general and specialized reference materials, as appropriate.

> L.5. Demonstrate understanding of figurative language, word relationships, and nuances in word meanings.

L.6. Acquire and use accurately a range of general academic and domain-specific words and phrases sufficient for reading, writing, speaking, and listening at the college and career readiness level; demonstrate independence in gathering vocabulary knowledge when considering a word or phrase important to comprehension or expression. (CCSSI 2010)

Language and Learning

To support the language learning needs of all young mathematicians, and particularly English language learners, we as instructors need to—

- "Understand the difference between conversational and academic language;

- "Identify, explicitly teach, and model the use of high-level academic vocabulary . . . that students need in order to understand our content; and

- "Recognize similarities and differences between English academic language and students' native languages; build from the similarities and make differences explicit and comprehensible" (Klaus-Quinlan and Nathanson-Mejía 2010, p. 18).

As noted by language acquisition researcher Jeff Zwiers (2006),

> Culturally and linguistically diverse students typically pick up social language rather quickly, and often appear to be "fluent" in English. However, being able to have a casual conversation does not guarantee that they are proficient in the academic language required to succeed in school. (Cited in Klaus-Quinlan and Nathanson-Mejía 2010, p. 18)

While we may be accustomed to considering only those children who speak a language other than English at home as English language learners, in fact, all youngsters in American schools are, in their own way, learners of English, as is each of us. To gain access to content knowledge, students need to develop an understanding of the academic language of that content area—both at the word level, as well as syntactically and structurally, as discussed in chapter 3.

Zwiers (2006) uses the term *academic language* to describe the way students and teachers talk with one another during learning time in school. Academic language includes—

- discourse patterns and phrases, such as "I respectfully disagree with you" or "We are going to analyze this approach" (the concept of discourse and the role of talk and collaboration are addressed more fully in chapter 5);

- modes of written and oral language specific to a content area, such as written proofs or discussions justifying a solution; and

- discipline-specific vocabulary, such as *estimate*, *reciprocal*, or *perpendicular*.

As math teachers, we need to heighten our awareness of those terms we use regularly in the context of discussing our content. As mathematical natives, we are steeped in the language of mathematics, ready to talk about coefficients over coffee or distribution plots over dinner; thus, we may suffer from a bit of expert blindness about which terms constitute academic language and which would be considered common parlance among the masses. Yet, for students to access the Common Core Standards for Mathematical Practice—to solve problems, argue, critique, and express—we need to explicitly teach, not just use, the academic language of our discipline.

To heighten your awareness of the incredible vocabulary load that mathematics demands, try this: Observe a colleague teaching for just one period. During that time, strive to jot down all the math-specific terms you hear out of her mouth. What do you notice? When we pay attention to the vast amount of vocabulary math learners need to understand, we can begin to appreciate the need for explicit vocabulary instruction.

Dead Word Cemetery

Teacher Deb Maruyama, featured in the vignette at the opening of this chapter, created a dead word cemetery on her classroom wall as a playful way to illuminate for her middle school math students, the majority of whom are academic English learners, the importance that she places on accuracy of academic speech. Early in the year, she and her students bury words such as *it* and *they* and *that*, writing odes to each and discussing why these vague pronouns will not support them in their math learning. Once dead, a word can no longer be used in class discussion. To a student stating, "I don't get it," Deb will reply, "'*It*' is dead," and then wait for the learner to rephrase her query with more specific language:

"I don't get how he got $x = 8$."

Now there is something to talk about.

Vocabulary Development for Math Learners

As a content area, mathematics includes a vocabulary all its own. A competent mathematician needs to understand words describing mathematical procedures, such as *calculate* and *graph*, as well as academic terms specific to mathematical content: *protractor*, *polygon*, and so forth. Further, many common English words, when used in mathematical contexts, have more specific meanings, such as *distribute, coordinate,* or *complementary*. Words, like numbers and symbols, are building blocks for students' mathematical reasoning.

To keep pace with their content learning in mathematics, students are expected to continually acquire new words to describe both the concepts they are studying and the processes they are performing. For math learners, a focus on acquisition of academic vocabulary has proven effective in boosting student achievement. Siegel (1989) offers this description:

> Direct teaching of the specialized vocabulary of mathematics contributes to improved success with problem solving. For example, Skrypa (1979) found that teaching mathematical vocabulary can improve students' ability to solve mathematical problems. The emphasis on the meaning as well as the decoding of words in this study is critical. Earp and Tanner (1980) found that sixth graders could decode but not give the meanings of mathematical terms commonly found in mathematics texts; however, students were able to give definitions when the terms were placed in the context of a sentence, leading the researchers to conclude that mathematical texts do not provide much support for comprehension. (pp. 6–7)

Though time spent developing students' rich grasp of mathematical terms may feel like a digression from math learning, vocabulary development in fact helps students deepen their conceptual understanding of our content area. Vocabulary knowledge is integral to the Common Core Standards for Mathematical Practice: To reason abstractly requires students to know the meanings of complex words, such as *ratio* or *parabolic*. To construct viable arguments requires students to be facile with the language of argument itself: *claim, evidence, reasoning*; to attend to precision requires students to grasp the fact that familiar words, such as *minute* or *mean*, have very specialized meanings in the context of math. Having power over words allows us to think more powerfully.

In this chapter, we will explore which words are worth studying and how vocabulary learning can be catalyzed within the context of the math workshop.

Which Words?

As you consider the imperative of vocabulary instruction, you may be thinking, "Ugh. If I stop every time I use a mathematical term to review its meaning and discuss, we will never get past chapter 1 all year long!" Understood. Given the overwhelming array of terms we could teach, we must strategically maximize any time devoted to vocabulary learning. Let's talk about which words are most critical to highlight so you can parcel out your vocabulary instruction efficiently and effectively.

According to language acquisition experts, vocabulary can be sorted into three levels, or tiers:

- Tier 1: The most basic words that are part of typical interpersonal communication. Tier 1 words require little instructional attention (*book, eat, slow*).

- Tier 2: Higher-frequency words found across a variety of domains, including functional or procedural words (*identify, evaluate*) as well as more complex synonyms for tier 1 words (*tome, consume, lethargic*). The Common Core State Standards refer to tier 2 words as "academic vocabulary"—words that students will encounter across disciplines. Figure 4.2 displays a list of all the tier 2 terms included in the Common Core State Standards for Mathematics.

- Tier 3: Lower-frequency, often content-specific, words (*isotope, exponent*). The Common Core State Standards refer to tier 3 words as "domain-specific vocabulary," the specialized terms of a given topic or discipline.

Traditional content-area vocabulary instruction has focused on tier 3 words through the study of definitions: Students memorize the meaning of terms such as *parallelogram, trapezoid*, and *dodecahedron* right before making mobiles of three-dimensional paper prisms, as I did decades ago as a geometry student. Yet recent research shows that our greatest return on investment comes from exploring the tier 2 words with learners, since this academic vocabulary is more relevant over the long term, draws on students' conceptual understanding, and can be used in a variety of ways.

This is not to say that tier 3 words can be ignored. Specialized terms, such as *summation, integral*, and *function*, are certainly a required part of our mathematical lexicon. Yet, we need to lay a foundation with the study of tier 2 words, since these are the language of learning, of thinking, and of school. We can build to tier 3 words from there.

adapt	design	plan
analyze	detect	present
apply	determine	probe
approximate	diagram	problem solve
argue	discern	reason
ask	distinguish	recognize
attend	estimate	record
build	evaluate	reflect
calculate	examine	relate
clarify	expand	repeat
classify	explain	represent
communicate	explore	respond
compare	express	revise
compose	form	search
comprehend	generalize	select
compute	generate	share
conceptualize	graph	shift
conclude	identify	simplify
conjecture	improve	solve
connect	interpret	sort
consider	justify	specify
construct	label	state
contextualize	listen	transform
convert	manipulate	understand
create	map	visualize
critique	measure	
decide	monitor	
decompose	navigate	
decontextualize	notice	
deepen	organize	
describe	preserve	

Fig. 4.2. Tier 2 procedural words in the Common Core State Standards for Mathematics

Familiar Words with Special Meaning in Math

Consider the following list of words found in our everyday language that take on unique meaning in the context of our discipline. What other words can you add to this list? How will you alert students to these words' math-specific definitions?

base	function	reciprocal
distribute	imaginary	series
factor	integral	unknown

Word roots

In addition to offering learners robust instruction around carefully selected terms, we support their lifelong vocabulary learning when we offer tools they can use independently and flexibly for dissecting technical language: knowledge of prefixes, suffixes and word roots.

Many of the academic terms in mathematics and science are derived from Greek and Latin roots. Time spent familiarizing students with those word parts can support learners in gaining access to a variety of terms with common prefixes or shared roots. Some teachers spend time with students teaching lists of roots, while others will discuss a word part when introducing a new term. Figure 4.3 lists a few common word parts to get you started. Numerous lists are available online for further exploration.

Root	Meaning	Examples
circum	around	circumference, circumscribe
cent	hundred	centimeter, percent
equi	equal	equilateral, equivalent
lat	side	lateral
meter	measure	kilometer
poly	many	polygon, polyhedron
quad	four	quadrant, quadrilateral
semi	half	semicircle, semiannual
tri	three	triangle, triple
uni	one	unilateral, unit

Fig. 4.3. Sample root words

Cognates

For all students, and especially English language learners, academic vocabulary development in mathematics involves a consciousness of cognates. Cognates are words that sound similar across languages. For example, in English we "find the difference," while in Spanish, we "encontra la diferencia." The words *difference* and *diferencia* sound similar enough that an astute language learner could infer the meaning of the English term from the Spanish, or vice versa, yet this is not an automatic operation for all. Direct instruction in the content classroom on identifying cognates and using first-language knowledge to discern their meaning honors and supports students who are bilingual or multilingual.

Not only can we use cognates to support learners' understanding of new terms as they are introduced, but we can also introduce students explicitly to the strategy of using cognates to infer meaning whenever they encounter unfamiliar words. But remind students to be cautious since this strategy does not always work: Some terms that sound similar do not mean the same thing at all.

Figure 4.4 includes a variety of math-related Spanish-English cognates. This language example was chosen because Spanish speakers currently comprise the majority of English language learners in American schools. Yet the strategy of using cognates to infer meaning is useful between any two languages. If you work with students of other language backgrounds, invite those learners to work with you to create math vocabulary cognate lists of their own.

angle	el ángulo	model	el modelo
absolute value	el valor absoluto	multiplication	la multiplicación
algebraic expression	la expresión algebraica	multiply	multiplicar
area	el área	negative number	el número negativo
bar graph	la gráfica de barros	number	el número
base	la base	number line	la línea numérica
center	el centro	numerator	el numerador
centimeter	el centímetro	parallel	paralelo/a (adjective)
circle	el círculo	parallelogram	el paralelogramo
circumference	la circunferencia	perimeter	el perímetro
common denominator	el denominador común	perpendicular	perpendicular
common factor	el factor común	pi	pi
congruent	congruente	polygon	el polígono
coordinates	las coordinadas	prediction	la predicción
cube	el cubo	prime number	el número primo
decimal	el decimal	probability	la probabilidad
denominator	el denominador	problem	el problema
diameter	el diámetro	product	el producto
difference	la diferencia	pyramid	la pirámide
different	diferente	quadrant	el cuadrante
digit	el dígito	quadrilateral	el cuadrilátero
divide	dividir	quotient	el cociente
equal	igual	radius	el radio
equation	la ecuación	range	el rango
equilateral	equilátero/a	reciprocal	recíproco/a (adjective)
equivalent	equivalente	rectangle	el rectángulo
estimate	estimar	reflection	la reflección
exponent	el exponente	regroup	reagrupar
expression	la expresión	results	los resultados
factor	el factor	rhombus	el rombo
Fahrenheit	Fahrenheit	seconds	los segundos
false	falso	segment	el segmento
function	la función	simplify	simplificar
graph	la gráfica	solution	la solución
hexagon	el hexágono	symmetry	la simetría

Fig. 4.4. Some English–Spanish math term cognates

horizontal	horizontal	table	la tabla
intersection	la intersección	temperature	la temperatura
isosceles	isósceles	total	el total
kilogram	el kilogramo	trapezoid	el trapezio
kilometer	el kilómetro	triangle	el triángulo
line	la línea	variable	la variable
line graph	la gráfica de líneas	vertex	el vértice
meter	el metro	vertical	vertical
millimeter	el milimetro	volume	el volumen
minute	el minuto	yard	la yarda
mixed number	el número mixto	zero	el cero
mode	el modo		

Fig. 4.4. *Continued*

Effective Vocabulary Instruction

How do you remember learning words in school? Copying definitions verbatim onto fold-ables? Drill and practice? An overview of the research on vocabulary instruction demonstrates that these traditional methods of teaching words are ineffective, that we can best support students' language acquisition with rich, frequent vocabulary instruction that introduces new terms as part of an interconnected web of meaning.

Myths about vocabulary learning

Introducing random words in isolation, expecting learners to acquire vocabulary by reading independently, or asking students to look up words in the dictionary (or online) is not as helpful as teachers of yore would have had us think. Even if those activities served you personally as a learner, there is strong evidence to suggest that other practices are more effective in promoting vocabulary development. But let's start by talking about what does not work, just to clear the air.

Isolation

Memorizing definitions, flipping through flash cards, and writing terms in sentences are all common, yet ineffective, vocabulary learning strategies. To build a web of understanding in their minds, learners need access to the rich interrelationships between terms and concepts, familiar and new (Daniels, Hyde, and Zemelman 2012).

Learning words through context

Wide reading is only marginally worthy as a means to grow vocabularies. Students acquire five to fifteen new words from every one hundred unfamiliar ones they meet as readers. To learn words from context, students must have the skills to infer word meaning from the text, must read widely enough to encounter a substantial number of unfamiliar words, and must read text of sufficient difficulty to present learning opportunities.

Dictionaries

Looking up words in the dictionary—even a mathematics dictionary—online or in a book can also be problematic. Typically, dictionaries offer limited differentiation between related terms, present definitions in vague language, offer multiple definitions with no guidance on how to select which is applicable to the circumstance, and are, in general, likely to be misinterpreted (Allen 1999). Try this: Imagine yourself as a beleaguered tenth grader struggling to understand the mathematical term *domain*. You look it up in Merriam-Webster's online dictionary and find the definitions below. How helpful is this?

1(a): complete and absolute ownership of land; (b): land so owned

2: a territory over which dominion is exercised

3: a region distinctively marked by some physical feature <the *domain* of rushing streams, tall trees, and lakes>

4: a sphere of knowledge, influence, or activity <the *domain* of art>

5: the set of elements to which a mathematical or logical variable is limited; *specifically:* the set on which a function is defined

6: any of the small randomly oriented regions of uniform magnetization in a ferromagnetic substance

7: integral domain

8: the highest taxonomic category in biological classification ranking above the kingdom

9: any of the three-dimensional subunits of a protein that are formed by the folding of its linear peptide chain and that together make up its tertiary structure

10: a subdivision of the Internet consisting of computers or sites usually with a common purpose (as providing commercial information) and denoted in Internet addresses by a unique abbreviation (as *com* or *gov*) (Merriam-Webster 2014)

Much of what may have been done unto you as a vocabulary learner, and perhaps some of what we may have done unto our vocabulary learning students in the past, has been shown to be either inefficient or ineffective. What, then, works?

Principles of effective vocabulary instruction

Particularly helpful to learners are instructional strategies that take them beyond word-definition memorization to engage them more fully with the concepts behind the terms (Harmon, Hedrick, and Wood 2005). Yet, since there will never be time enough in any subject area in school to directly teach all the vocabulary students need in that content area, learners need more than piles of terms stacked in their brains. They also need to acquire strategies for *how* to learn words, such as using context clues or drawing on knowledge of word roots.

Highly effective vocabulary instruction goes beyond teaching the meaning of each individual word and instead engages learners with rich, rapid exposure to new words, linking those terms as part of an interconnected web of concepts.

To offer vocabulary instruction at this level, we limit how many words we work with at one time: five new words a week, taught richly, will advance learners' vocabularies far more than twenty terms glossed over in the same time frame. Figure 4.5 orients us to key principles of effective vocabulary instruction, why they matter, and how we can put them into practice.

What Learners Need to Understand Vocabulary Deeply

- A meaningful context: a reason to care about the word(s)

- Student-friendly explanations: descriptions of concepts in students' own words

- Multiple contexts and frequent exposure: opportunities to play with terms in a variety of ways and settings spread across a series of days

- Numerous interactions: chances to talk about and engage with the term(s) orally, kinesthetically, graphically, and in read and written language

- Frequent exposures: times to explore the new words at least every day for a week

What	Why	How
Frame words in a meaningful context	Allows learners to make connections among ideas	Introduce and discuss terms within a math lesson, rather than as a separate activity. Invite learners to relate new terms to prior knowledge.
Go beyond the study of definitions to include active engagement with word meanings	To actively engage, learners need to think and respond, and this cements their understanding.	See "Word Interaction Ideas" in figure 4.8.
Invite learners to represent words in their own linguistic and nonlinguistic ways	Gives learners an opportunity to "own" the terms, make them their own	Ask students to develop their own definitions (as modeled by Deb Maruyama's students above), as well as to create visual or kinesthetic representations that remind them of the term's meaning.
Involve students in the gradual shaping of word meanings through multiple exposures in various contexts	Can build understanding when introducing a new word by spending time engaging learners with it daily for at least a week	Facilitate discussions, games, activities, competitions, or other interactions; "quick and frequent" works better than "exhaustive and isolated."
Teach word parts to enhance students' capacities to understand new terms	Enhances students' abilities to make meaning of other technical terms later on	Break apart new words looking for familiar prefixes, suffixes and roots; use these as opportunities to discuss and explore new word parts (see list in fig. 4.3).

Fig. 4.5. Effective vocabulary instruction

Principles into practice

So, what does this really look like? Imagine devoting just a few minutes during each class period to explicitly focusing on vocabulary development. This activity can be embedded within the mini-lesson of your math workshop, presented as a "catch" during learners' work time, or otherwise integrated as an interconnected part of math instruction. Each segment of vocabulary instruction is intentional, planned, and linked to the prior day's and the next day's vocabulary learning.

In one study (Marzano 2004), six-step vocabulary instruction was found to increase student achievement by 24 percentage points. Participating teachers followed a very structured, six-step approach:

1. Provide description, explanation, example.

2. Ask students to restate the description, explanation, or example in their own words.

3. Ask students to construct a picture, pictograph, or symbolic representation of the term.

4. Engage students periodically in activities that help them add to their knowledge of the terms in their vocabulary notebooks.

5. Periodically ask students to discuss the terms with one another.

6. Involve students periodically in games that enable them to play with terms. (Marzano 2004)

In the context of math instruction, we might condense those six steps into three:

1. Identify critical unit vocabulary and plan for instruction.

2. Introduce and record terms, a few at a time.

3. Actively engage with vocabulary on a daily basis.

Identify critical unit vocabulary and plan for instruction

As described in the discussion of which words are the most critical to highlight, we best support learners by focusing on tier 2 words, as well as on critical concepts from tier 3. As you prepare to teach a unit, scan your instructional materials to select the most important terms that students will need to master to succeed; go beyond simply adopting the vocabulary list in the teacher's guide, and consider including procedural terms from the Common Core list above, or other important tier 2 words.

For example, in preparing to teach a unit on slope, a teacher might be tempted to include the following vocabulary terms on her week 1 list: *equation*, *slope*, *y-intercept*, and *coefficient*, all of which are indeed integral to learners' understanding of slope. Yet, consider the tier 2 words that might come before these discipline-specific terms: *graph*, *represent*, and *visualize*, as well as the common English words whose special meanings are important in the context of this lesson: *line*, for one, as well as *rise* and *run*. See figure 4.6 for an example of how one teacher stretched tier 2 and tier 3 vocabulary instruction across a three-week unit on slope.

As you plan, keep the vocabulary list short, just a handful of words a week, knowing that you will need time to revisit the terms from the previous week at intervals as well.

And don't worry about covering everything; you will have other units across the year in which to teach additional vocabulary.

Once you have identified the words to focus on, spread them across the weeks of that unit, planning to address about five new words per week. (This is *not* one per day but rather an introduction of a handful of words per week, to be introduced and revisited throughout that week and beyond.)

Week	Tier 2 terms	Tier 3 terms/common terms with math-specific meanings
1	graph, represent	equation, line, slope
2	interpret, visualize	negative, positive, rise, run
3	compare, describe	coefficient, function, unit rate, *y*-intercept

Fig. 4.6. Sample plan for vocabulary instruction: Slope

Once you have identified which words you want to teach when, make a plan for instruction of each. For each word, take some time to consider these questions:

- What background knowledge might students have about this word?
- What other terms are related?
- Is this a cognate?

Depending on your answers, you can decide how you will introduce and illuminate each term.

Introduce and record terms

Having carefully selected the vocabulary that students need to master each week, devote instructional time to introducing those words, supporting students in weaving their new understanding into the web of their prior knowledge.

Introducing a term may take a bit of time. Create opportunities for students to grasp the meaning by offering numerous multi-modal examples to illustrate each term. These might include—

- images;
- short videos;
- realia (objects from the physical world);
- stories;
- skits; and
- music.

Let's listen in as Ms. Garcia introduces the term *slope* to seventh graders during her mini-lesson:

"Here's a very important term in this unit, *slope*. Let me hear you say it, *slope*."

"Slope!" the class replies in enthusiastic chorus.

"Now, what do you think that means?" Some hands shoot into the air, while a few students' eyes roll to their shoes. "Let's give each other a moment to think this over . . . Now, turn and talk to your shoulder partner. What is slope? If you are not sure, talk about what you think it might be."

Students shuffle to arrange themselves face-to-face with partners, and then the quiet hum of thinking and sharing fills the air. After about 90 seconds, Ms. Garcia gathers the class's attention with her chime and starts to call on students (in this case, "warm calling," as described in chapter 5): "What did you and your partner discuss?" She records their responses with a list on the interactive board:

- A hill
- Where you ski
- How steep something is
- A slant

No one responds with an algebraic definition, but the shared ideas illustrate that the learners have some background knowledge of the general concept. "All of this is absolutely correct! In typical conversation, this is exactly what we mean by slope—a hill or the slant of something." Ms. Garcia then shows and discusses just a few slides, reminding learners of the common definition of slope: a picture of a steep road with a sign indicating the gradient, an image of a ski hill, one of a mountainside jutting up from the sea. Students respond to the images with interest.

From here, Ms. Garcia layers in the mathematical meaning of the term. "Now in mathematics, slope has a very specific meaning, one that we are going to be exploring for the next few weeks. Slope is defined by mathematicians as 'the steepness and direction of a line.' Think about that for a moment. What do you think they mean?"

Ms. Garcia invites learners to respond to her query and then further explains the mathematical definition with graphic illustrations and examples on the board. After a few minutes, she asks learners to pull out their math notebooks and record, each in his or her own words, how they would describe the meaning of *slope* in common conversation, as well as mathematicians' definition of the term.

Documenting Vocabulary Learning

Many teachers find it helpful to create systems and structures for learners to document new words. Students understand terms more deeply when asked to record definitions in their own words, to sketch visual reminders that make sense to them, and to provide their own examples, rather than copy a given summary of a term (see fig. 4.5). Here are a few places where learners might record vocabulary:

- A section in their math notebook (discussed further in chapter 6)
- A stand-alone glossary
- A graphic organizer (such as that in fig. 4.7)
- Index cards, one per word, clipped together with a binder ring

Any structure will do, yet students will develop a strong routine of recording and referring to their vocabulary collections if we sustain a consistent format for recording from unit to unit.

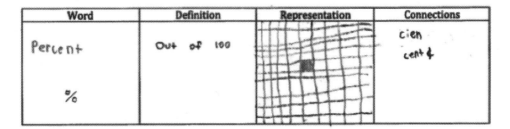

Fig. 4.7. Student work sample: Vocabulary list

Resources for Vocabulary Instruction Ideas

Bringing Words to Life: Robust Vocabulary Instruction, by Isabel L. Beck, Margaret G. McKeown, and Linda Kucan

Building Academic Vocabulary: Teachers' Manual, by Robert Marzano and Debra Pickering

Classroom Instruction That Works for English Language Learners, by Jane D. Hill and Kathleen M. Flynn

Words, Words, Words: Teaching Vocabulary, in Grades 4–12, by Janet Allen

---

Actively engage

Introducing and recording terms is just the beginning. From here, learners need time to develop their own conceptual understanding. We serve them when we create daily opportunities, however brief, for interaction with new terms. Discussion, art, kinesthetic activities, and quick games can all be integrated into the work time of our math workshops. Figure 4.8 introduces some activities that will get learners engaged in articulating the nuances of new vocabulary. Riff on these to create your own.

Activity	Description	Example
Conversation (for pairs, small groups, or whole-class discussion)		
Word associations	Ask students to associate a known word with a new word. Go beyond synonyms to deal with relationships.	"What is the relationship between *creating* and *critiquing*?"
Ranking importance	Ask students to decide which concept is more critical.	"What is more important, *estimating* or *calculating*, and why?
Would you rather . . . ?	Ask students to compare one term with another and declare a preference, with a rationale.	"Would you rather ride your bike around a curve shaped like a *parabola* or a *hyperbola*? Why?"
Have you ever . . . ?	Ask students to associate words with contexts and experiences from their lives.	"Have you ever used an *obtuse angle*?"

Fig. 4.8. Word interaction ideas

Activity	Description	Example
Creativity		
Concept map	Sketch and label a web illustrating the interrelationships among terms.	Put each of these terms—*mean, median, mode,* and *range*—in its own circle. Where you see a relationship between two terms, draw a line and describe that relationship in writing.
Sculptures	Using modeling dough, create a three-dimensional representation of the term.	Make a *hexagon* . . . A *right triangle* . . .
Kinesthetic		
Applause, applause!	Students are asked to clap to indicate how much they'd like to act on a tier 2 word (and why or why not).	Try . . . *Compare* *Compose* *Compute*
Lineups	Imagining the length of the room as a number line, place yourself on that continuum on the basis of your level of confidence in your ability to . . .	*Evaluate,* then *Examine,* then *Explain*
Statues	Hold your body in a way that represents the term.	Be a *rhombus.* Be a *line with a slope of zero.*
Games		
Pictionary	Invite a learner to silently draw a term while classmates guess the term.	Try . . . *Divide*
Apples to Apples	As in the commercially produced game, students associate nouns with adjectives and vie and argue for the closest association.	Adjective: *huge* Noun choices: *infinity, googol, infinitesimal*
Jeopardy	You know the TV quiz show. Take some index cards and make your own.	

Fig. 4.8. *Continued*

With a smattering of these activities spread across each week, each unit, each set of words, students gain multiple opportunities to develop their own understanding of the terms. Interspersed with these interactions can be moments of reflection and synthesis. As learners play and practice, invite them to revisit the place where they recorded their new words and add to their thinking and understanding, noticing their deepening grasp of each concept at hand.

Words Are Worth Working For

The English language is vast; for students, the academic language of mathematics holds the key to their future success. To scaffold all learners' mathematical language acquisition, we need to teach words explicitly. We begin by selecting the terms to address and then plan for instruction that is interactive and engaging, offering learners multiple exposures to new words across time, along with opportunities to record their understanding. In these ways, we support students in developing vocabulary as an interconnected web of ideas.

Word Walls

The word wall—a place where unit vocabulary terms are posted visibly—has become a popular feature in classrooms across content areas. Word walls can look pretty, especially if you use colored paper and nice, large fonts. But beware: Word walls do very little to advance students' vocabulary learning unless we make them both helpful and interactive.

Helpful word walls are those that are organized conceptually and include scaffolds for understanding. To this end, rather than scattering terms across a bulletin board, we can organize them in a way that makes sense conceptually so that learners can see the interrelationships among the concepts. Effective word walls include not only the words but also visual representations and context clues that help students to understand and remember their meaning: drawings, diagrams, and artifacts. These can be created by students and posted, along with the terms, to support their comprehension and retention (Jackson, Tripp, and Cox 2011).

Helpful word walls also include a mix of both academic vocabulary (tier 2) and domain-specific vocabulary (tier 3). The tier 2 terms remain and expand over the course of the year, while the tier 3 words can change, unit by unit.

Interactive word walls are more of a living resource than a static display. The best word walls are co-created by students and teachers; this is the first level of interaction. From there, learners can continually engage with the wall by adding material, referring to it in their work, playing games that engage them with the wall and the terms, and revisiting the graphic layout of the words as they refine their understanding. In this way, the word wall becomes a living resource that students can consult to help them understand and remember.

In this chapter, you have read a variety of word lists and encountered a collection of strategies that invite learners to engage with words. These can serve as a starting place in your planning for explicit vocabulary instruction linked to content learning every day. This emphasis will not only increase students' abilities to engage in meaningful mathematical discourse but also build their conceptual understanding, as described by NCTM's *Principles to Actions* (2014). Above all, your careful attention to vocabulary instruction will expand horizons and open doors. As twentieth-century philosopher Ludwig Wittgenstein (1922) said, "The limits of my language mean the limits of my world." You are opening students' worlds to unlimited possibilities with words.

"Yeah, but . . . "

- *"I've tried teaching vocab, but students don't remember the words anyway."*

The more time and energy we devote to robust, engaging vocabulary instruction that presents words as relevant and related, the more likely students will be to remember the terms across time. Engage individuals in a process of reflecting on what they know helps them to remember; encourage them to take responsibility for their own learning, applying energy to practicing those strategies they personally find most helpful.

- *"The need is so great. How can I stick with just a handful of words at a time?"*

Less is more. Though it may be tempting to layer a dozen words a week into our instruction, research suggests that fewer words, learned deeply through thoughtful interaction, are more likely to stick than a long list of words sparsely examined. Strive to stick with five to eight new words each week. Trust that students have many more opportunities and avenues to continue this learning.

- *"How do I differentiate, since some students know a lot of these words already?"*

Even when students "know" a word, they may not be familiar with its nuances and applications in all contexts, so we can engage students in a conversation about what it means to "know." Receptive language skills (what we hear and understand) often far exceed expressive language skills (what we say). Encourage all learners to actively use new vocabulary every week in new ways and to stretch their own limits in language acquisition.

 **Vocabulary Instruction Planning Template**

Engaging in Mathematical Discourse to Deepen Understanding

All learning floats on a sea of talk.

—James Britton, *Language and Learning*

Problems of the Day

- Why talk about math?

- How can we structure productive mathematical discourse?

Kathy Sampson's Algebra 1 students are working in small groups to develop equations for lines of their own that are parallel to the line $5 + 2x = y$. Let's take a quick look inside the classroom as the students work:

Kelsie:	0, 5, and 10 are on a y-intercept, and so that will get us a parallel line.
Tianna:	I see where you're going with that. I'm just a little confused on what we're going to do with that, so could you explain it a little bit more?
Kelsie:	If we changed the equation, could $y = 5 + 2x$ work?
Tom:	But $5 + 2x$ is starting at the same point as this one.
Shane:	It would intercept at some point. We have to make it far enough down.
Ms. Sampson:	What was your original equation?
Tianna:	She said $5 + 2x = y$.
Tom:	That wouldn't work because that's starting at the same point.
Ms. Sampson:	What can you infer from that?

Kelsie: That we have to change the starting number, too.

Ms. Sampson: What did you infer from disproving this?

Shane: Can't we just make it 10 + 6x?

Kelsie: Let's make a table for that.

This is just a taste of math discourse; we will hear more from this lesson later in the chapter.

What Is Mathematical Discourse?

Discourse is engaged, accountable conversation and collaboration about thinking that cultivates understanding. It is more than just "talk." Discourse is mathematical thinkers' active effort to make sense by discussing ideas with others. You know it when you hear it. Discourse engages learners, promotes mathematical understanding, develops communication skills, and supports language development (Hoffer 2012). It can also be loud, chaotic, and difficult to channel. To get students collaborating as mathematicians requires coordination and faith. In this chapter, we will explore how and why to muster both.

If your own middle and high school math classes looked anything like the ones I attended, you spent a lot of time listening to the teacher talk and were sometimes put on the spot to respond to a question and were then told whether you were right or wrong. This old-school discourse pattern is known as IRE: the teacher *initiates*, a single student *responds*, and the teacher *evaluates* that response (Cazden 2001).

Despite its solid footing in classrooms across the nation even today, IRE is not a pattern of classroom talk that promotes collective thinking and understanding. To develop learners' meaning making as mathematicians, we must instead shift to a style of discourse that puts students and their collective thinking at the center of all conversation.

Warm Calling: A Scaffold for Discourse

We all need a moment to think. Too often, pressed for time, teachers expect instant feedback from learners: turn and talk, raise your hand and speak, thumbs up if you know the answer. Yet research indicates that students fare far better both in developing their understanding and honing their ability to articulate that understanding when we actually give them the gift of time just to think.

To this end, I suggest cultivating a habit of warm calling in your classroom. You cold call when you stun a student by suddenly calling on him to cough up an answer. By contrast, you warm call when you give everyone some uninterrupted, low-pressure time to warm up—sit and think, stop and jot—before anyone needs to say anything. Silence for a minimum of five full seconds of wait time. Try it. Then call on whomever you like. You may find, as researchers did, that learners will come up with more complex responses, as well as link their responses to the comments of others (Rowe 1986).

The Absolute Value of Discourse

Discourse is a key facet of intellectual development. Learners' understanding grows through opportunities to speak and listen to one another. As Vygotsky (1978) well knew, students are capable of ascending far steeper challenges in teams than they might individually. Vygotsky's theory of a zone of proximal development rests on the premise that with social support, through conversation, students expand their capacities at a rate far faster than they could alone.

For this reason, NCTM's Mathematics Teaching Practices highlight discourse as one of eight critical instructional approaches to promote students' mathematical understanding:

> **Facilitate meaningful mathematical discourse.** Effective teaching of mathematics facilitates discourse among students to build shared understanding of mathematical ideas by analyzing and comparing student approaches and arguments. (NCTM 2014)

Mathematical knowledge has a long history of being socially constructed. When we invite learners to share ideas and respond to the thinking of peers, we are welcoming them into the culture of mathematicians. Being able to speak and listen as mathematicians is one component of the disciplinary literacy of math.

In his recent study of the impact of peer-assisted reflection (PAR) on calculus students' learning, Daniel Reinholz (2014) found significant positive gains for learners who engaged in a cycle of independent work on a challenging problem, reflection on their own work, a conversation with a student partner about the problem, and finally revision of their own work. Not only were participating learners' work completion rates higher than those of students in the control group (98% vs. 70.2%), but the PAR group also had a significantly higher success rate in the course (23% higher than the control group). Participating students responded positively to their experience with PAR. One student, Mike, explained his response:

> PAR is good. I like how we can put our initial solution down, and even if it's wrong it doesn't really matter, because we can just talk about it with a group member the next day, and figure it out together. And generally you don't get stuck on a wrong solution, you figure it out. (Reinholz 2014)

By structuring peer feedback, training learners to have productive conversations, and matching them randomly for those discussions, Reinholz saw significant positive academic gains in what is typically a grueling course that filters many students out of college math and science opportunities. Discourse made a difference.

For English language learners in particular, discourse plays a key role in supporting language development, facilitating comprehension, and promoting life skills. Researcher Jeff Zwiers (whose ideas you may recall from our focus on vocabulary in chapter 4), and his colleagues explain:

> Particularly in schools with large numbers of academic English learners, lessons have focused on building up the skills and knowledge of each individual student. Students have been asked to focus much of their learning time on independent practice in preparation for tests. The Common Core State Standards, on the other hand, value the skills of communication and collaboration, which are both the goals and the means for achieving other learning objectives. The better students get at negotiating and explaining content ideas, the better they learn them. The better students get at communication, the better prepared they are for communicating in college, careers, and life. (Zwiers, O'Hara, and Pritchard 2014, p. 9)

In addition to discourse being fertile ground for the growth of all learners' understanding and ideas, discourse is also a useful stepping-stone to writing (which will be discussed further in chapter 6). Through opportunities for oral rehearsal of their thinking, learners cue up both the concepts they want to share and the academic language they need to express those ideas. For this reason, any writing task can be supported by a preparatory conversation.

Discourse and the Common Core

The Common Core not only presents standards for speaking and listening in language arts but also illuminates in the Mathematical Practices the value of discussion in mathematics. Discourse is integral to the achievement of the following practices:

1. Make sense of problems and persevere in solving them.

2. Reason abstractly and quantitatively.

3. Construct viable arguments and critique the reasoning of others. (CCSSI 2010)

To achieve these practices, students are going to need to communicate with one another productively and efficiently. The CCSS shift to emphasize problem solving, reasoning, and argument in mathematics will, in some cases, require fundamental changes to our instructional practice: We need to give learners something interesting to talk about.

Practicing routine procedures offers limited scope for the kinds of conversation invited by the Common Core (see fig. 5.1). To respond to these new standards, to generate student discourse that promotes mathematical understanding, we need to offer learners tasks of high cognitive demand and facilitate them in a way that sustains that level of rigor (NCTM 2014). With complex tasks that invite rich thinking as a starting point, we can engage learners in fruitful discourse. (For further resources on locating and creating tasks of high cognitive demand, see the appendix.)

Comprehension and Collaboration

   1. Prepare for and participate effectively in a range of conversations and collaborations with diverse partners, building on others' ideas and expressing their own clearly and persuasively.

   2. Integrate and evaluate information presented in diverse media and formats, including visually, quantitatively, and orally.

   3. Evaluate a speaker's point of view, reasoning, and use of evidence and rhetoric.

Presentation of Knowledge and Ideas

   4. Present information, findings, and supporting evidence such that listeners can follow the line of reasoning and the organization, development, and style are appropriate to task, purpose, and audience.

   5. Make strategic use of digital media and visual displays of data to express information and enhance understanding of presentations.

   6. Adapt speech to a variety of contexts and communicative tasks, demonstrating command of formal English when indicated or appropriate.

Fig. 5.1. College and Career Readiness Anchor Standards for Speaking and Listening (CCSSI 2010)

What Does Mathematical Discourse Sound Like?

Almost like a great song, top-notch mathematical discourse is something you know when you hear it. Yet, to cultivate quality, you and your students need a vision—or an "ausion" (a word I just made up to describe an ideal auditory vision)—of what you're going after. As described by Jeremy Kilpatrick and colleagues,

> Mathematics classrooms are more likely to be places in which mathematical proficiency develops when they are communities of learners and not collections of isolated individuals. Research on creating classrooms that function as communities of learners has identified several important features of these classrooms: ideas and methods are valued, students have autonomy in choosing and sharing solution methods, mistakes are valued as sites for learning for everyone, and the authority for correctness lies in logic and the structure of the subject, not the teacher. (Kilpatrick, Swafford, and Findell 2001, p. 425)

Three attributes stand out in any classroom where I hear the hum of powerful student discourse. Conversations are—

- respectful;
- student led; and
- rich with academic and domain-specific vocabulary.

Let's listen in to identify each attribute in action.

Discourse is respectful

"I would respectfully disagree with Shanae because I think the square root of 136 would have to be between 11 and 12. What do you all think?"

In classrooms that invite discourse, students take responsibility for their own learning and for supporting the learning of others. They focus their conversations on ideas, not personalities, and are supportive and collegial in discussion. Learners give and receive feedback, relishing opportunities to grow their thinking. Rather than saying "What?" and "I don't get it!" they may use phrases such as these:

- I am wondering . . .
- Could you explain . . .
- I agree (or disagree) with ____ because . . .

These conversation patterns take time to develop and require explicit teaching of academic vocabulary (see chapter 4). When such discourse patterns are in place, they evolve from what Peter Johnston (2004) calls the dynamic-learning belief system: Students see themselves and their classmates as works in progress, capable of revising their thinking and growing their understanding in light of new evidence. This respect for self and others is cultivated by conscientious teacher talk targeting students' sense of agency and flexibility.

Discourse is student led

"That does not make sense to me. Can you say more?"

"Sure, my idea is that since 11 squared is 121 and 12 squared is 144, and 136 is in between . . ."

When learners engage in discourse, they lead the conversation, posing questions of one another that probe for thinking: "How?" "Why?" They listen and respond to the inquiries of their peers by explaining drawings, defending solutions, justifying answers, or expanding thinking. Learners take responsibility by asking questions when they are lost, and they know that it is their job to explain effectively to allay the confusion of their peers.

The teacher facilitates patiently from the periphery, stepping in only as needed to propel the conversation forward. Posing purposeful questions, one of the NCTM's Mathematical Teaching Practices, offers us an opportunity to "assess and advance students' reasoning and sense making about important mathematical ideas and relationships" (NCTM 2014).

Discourse is rich with academic and domain-specific vocabulary

"So, you are explaining that because 11 to the exponent 2 is 121, and 12 squared is 144, and 136 is in between those two perfect squares, its square root needs to be between their square roots, between 11 and 12?"

Students engaged in high-level math discourse speak in complete sentences, using academic vocabulary as well as domain-specific mathematical terminology to describe their thinking. They avoid general pronouns, such as *it* or *they*, and instead refer to "the triangle on the left," and "my table group, Estella and Marco." As emphasized in chapter 4, regular interaction with and use of tier 2 and tier 3 terms scaffolds students' understanding, and for this reason, vigilant teachers encourage and promote precision of language during students' discourse.

We can cultivate students' fluency with academic and domain-specific language with our relentless and compassionate insistence on accuracy of speech. To this end, we are willing to stop a student mid-conversation and ask him to rephrase: "'That?' What is the 'that'?" Though this habit can temporarily divert the conversation, it signals to all listening the value of precision. Common Core Standard for Mathematical Practice 6 calls on us to "Attend to precision" (CCSSI 2010). This recommendation can refer not only to precision in calculations, but also to precision of language.

As we insist, students will test us, but if we hold true to high standards and offer support within our math workshops, learners' language will rise to meet our highest expectations.

Teaching Discourse in a Math Workshop

A math workshop is an excellent forum for inviting learners to engage in discourse. With a mini-lesson focused on introducing some key content, a generative task, structures for conversation throughout the work time, a steady rhythm of catch and release oscillating from small- to large-group conversation, and time reserved for reflecting and solidifying thinking, talk can be the medium for both engagement and understanding. Let's listen.

Mini-lesson: Refresh and build background knowledge for the conversation

Kathy Sampson's Algebra 1 students are exploring parallel and perpendicular lines. First, she invites all learners to record the learning target in their notebooks. (For more on math notebooks, and on the importance of writing in math, see chapter 6.) Kathy then launches the day-starter question: "So, what are *parallel* and *perpendicular*? What do they look like? You can draw me diagrams, ask me questions, write sentences. Tell me what you know. Give me your background knowledge right now."

After giving the students a few minutes of silent writing time, she calls the group back together: "Try to finish up in the next fifteen seconds or so." Then she invites learners to engage in table conversations. "What I want you to do in your groups is to talk about parallel and perpendicular."

Students begin to speak:

"They will never intersect each other. They will just go like this." (The student gestures with parallel arms.)

"I don't exactly know what perpendicular are. They are sort of like parallel."

"I thought of RR tracks. I don't think they cross, but they go in any direction."

"Straight lines."

When the teacher calls the students' attention from their table-group discussions and reconvenes the group for whole-group sharing, one student scribe hops to the board and records.

"Our group said perpendicular lines are lines that cross."

"They have to have opposite slopes."

"They have to have a right angle."

"Our group had a misconception. We had that they never cross. But now that I am hearing what other groups say, I see a difference."

After some further sharing and conversation, Kathy draws the discussion to a close. "What questions do you have for me about what *parallel* and *perpendicular* mean? We have to know what those mean to write equations." She clarifies in response to students' questions and then launches them into their work.

Work time: Give them something rich to talk about

"You ready?" asks Kathy. "Your task: Find a line that is parallel to the line $y = 5 + 3x$ and write the equation of the line. Task 2: Find a line that is perpendicular to $y = 5 + 3x$, and look for patterns.

"There are a lot of resources in this room. You can use graph paper. The only resource that's not available to you is to Google. So, while I pass out papers, pencils down; I want you to verbalize one idea about how you are going to do this."

Learners begin discussing, "I want to graph some of the points in that first line."

"I like that idea, and I think if we are going to make a graph, we should first make a table."

"What are we going to go up to with our table then?" The students get started making a table based on the equation.

Moving along, another peer probes, "I see where you are going with that. I am just a little confused on what we are going to do with that, so could you explain it a little bit more?" Students work and work, applying various strategies in different groups. Soon, a shout of glee comes from one corner: "We made it parallel! I did it, thanks to you guys."

Sharing and reflection: Bring ideas together

Kathy calls the groups back together with an invitation to share: "Tell me the patterns that you saw and the generalizations that you made."

"I think the pattern was we kept $3x$ the same, and we doubled the y-intercept. The y-intercept doubled, but the coefficient stayed the same."

"Yeah, I agree with that."

"Our group noticed that both lines have to have the same slope."

"I agree with Augie. To have a line that's parallel to the one given, both slopes need to be the same."

"We thought at first you had to double each one, the y-intercept and the slope, and tried $10 + 6x$, but we realized that they wouldn't be parallel so you had to keep it $3x$."

Reflect

Compare and contrast the student discourse in Kathy Sampson's classroom with your students' discourse. What is something to celebrate in your students' ability to collaborate to make sense of math? On the basis of Kathy's example, where might you push your students next?

The remarks above are verbatim quotes from students, and a visit to Kathy Sampson's classroom would offer you many more opportunities to hear learners speaking as mathematicians engaged in academic discourse. Yet this culture of thinking did not arise all on its own; in fact, there was a time when most students in the room were mute. Yet with dogged determination, Kathy intentionally cultivated a community of thinkers ready to speak and listen as mathematicians every day. How can we entice learners to engage in conversation of this caliber?

Generative Topics

"What did you get for number 6?"

"Five pi."

"Me, too."

"Cool."

"Cool."

Generative Topics, *continued*

Not much to discuss there. To engage in vibrant mathematical discussions, students need something truly rich to talk about—not worksheets, not right answers, but controversy. To this end, researcher Jeff Zwiers (2007) describes five sorts of discourse that promote language development for academic English learners and can guide us to tee up rich conversations for all students. Zwiers challenges us to consider how we might ask math learners to engage in these types of discourse:

- Identify cause and effect
- Compare
- Interpret
- Take multiple perspectives
- Persuade with evidence

Classroom Culture Cultivates Mathematical Discourse

"A significant amount of class time should be spent in developing mathematical ideas and methods rather than only practicing skills," state Kilpatrick, Swafford, and Findell in the National Research Council publication *Adding It Up* (2001). To this end, classroom discourse provides fertile ground for the discussion of ideas and strategies that lead to mathematical understanding.

Wrangling tweens and teens into conscientious conversations about mathematical thinking is no small task. Students may show up with a lot of other topics they would rather talk about, or they may have been habituated over years of schooling not to speak in class at all. Creating a classroom culture rich in mathematical discourse requires deliberate effort over time. By adopting an egalitarian stance, setting norms, modeling, providing scaffolds, offering feedback, and holding learners accountable, teachers can effectively cultivate high-quality discourse among learners of all stripes.

Standing for discourse

A prerequisite to student discourse is a teacher's willingness to give up control of the conversation in the classroom. To step away from the traditional IRE pattern so common in classrooms and instead let learners "own" the conversation requires a fundamental shift in our perception of our role, from dispensers of information to coaches of thinking. It requires trusting students, the power of their ideas, and the strength of their voices to explain, convince, and teach one another.

When we invite students to engage in discourse, we do not get to decide what gets said. Instead of telling, we need to listen and facilitate; instead of offering a rationale, we need to probe learners for a justification; instead of sweeping away every crumb of confusion with our own instantaneous and sturdy explanations, we need to let learners linger there, to dig deep, share their thinking, build on the thinking of others until they can achieve clarity for themselves.

To this end, Peter Johnston (2012) suggests the following strategies for conveying your confidence in students and their capacity to lead the thinking in the room.

- Ask open-ended questions: "Why do you think . . . ?" and not "What would x be?"

- Use uncertainty markers: "maybe," "perhaps," "I wonder."

- Offer wait time. Count to ten in your head before calling on anyone. Ever.

- Don't judge ideas. Say, "Hmm. What do you all think of this?" and not "Good! Right!"

- Arrange for class members to manage turn-taking without you.

- Let learners speak for themselves. Do not repeat students' good ideas so the class can hear them.

- Ask students to report to the class what their partner had to say rather than what they themselves had to say.

- Remind students to speak directly to each other rather than through you.

Resisting the Temptation to Tell

As Margaret Smith (2000, p. 382) pointed out, "Most tasks that promote reasoning and problem solving take time to solve, and frustration may occur, but perseverance in the face of initial difficulty is important."

As adults, we know a lot—a whole lot. We are good at explaining. We are right. But telling learners everything does not help them to become independent problem solvers. We cannot rescue students from struggle. Our expertise can undermine classroom discourse. In his well-titled article "Never Say Anything a Kid Can Say," teacher Steven Reinhart (2000) describes how he shifted from a teacher-centered to a student-centered classroom: "My definition of a good teacher has since changed from 'one who explains things so well that students understand' to 'one who gets students to explain things so well that they can be understood'" (p. 54).

To cultivate classroom discourse, we as teachers can begin to listen more than we speak, to ask far more than we tell, and to be willing to let learners be uncomfortable in their uncertainty. Your mettle will be tested when student confusion arises. Acknowledge it, inquire about it, but bite your tongue lest you explain away a learner's opportunity to grapple with uncertainty and win understanding.

Setting norms

How do you need and want students to be together as learners to promote generative discourse? Rather than rules, let's call these ideas "norms," because norms refer to the ways in which colleagues collectively agree to engage with one another, while rules are handed down by an authority who is ready to dole out consequences for missteps.

To develop norms for discourse, you and your students might spend time brainstorming about how the class will engage in learning-focused conversations. Or just go ahead and pen a poster yourself explaining how productive communities of learners behave in general, as well as participate in discourse in particular. Then invite learners to discuss and revise your proposed norms. Here are a few basics you could include:

- Look at and listen to the speaker.

- Be thinking and ready to respond.

- Use respectful language.

- Use academic language.

- Share the air. (Don't dominate the conversation.)

Modeling

Once you have established norms, model them, practice them, notice them, and name them. We might expect that all secondary students know what a "turn and talk" looks like, but reminders never hurt. Show them a good example: Face the speaker, respond with your voice, take turns. Show them a crummy example: Turn away, remain mum, or dominate the conversation. Let the students observe and then rip the example apart. Even though we think teen students should know these things already, learners benefit from clear expectations that in this classroom, this is what these norms look like. Be willing to revisit and model again as needed.

Another way to reinforce norms is to refer learners to peer models. Notice and name successful engagement. Identify specific behaviors that students adopted and how those are serving their learning: "Wow, I see Ava facing her partner, listening carefully, and jotting ideas in her notebook. The close attention she is paying to the speaker will help her to respond to his thinking when it is her turn to speak." Acknowledging peer exemplars, rather than expending energy on firefighting isolated unfortunate behavior, can offer positive reinforcement to the entire group.

Scaffolding with sentence starters

Some students come to class ready to talk, while others may have grown used to sitting through math with their voices turned off. To channel all students into productive conversation, some scaffolds may be helpful. Try sentence stems. They can be posted on a wall, taped to a table, recorded in learners' notebooks, or distributed on a handout. A generic list of go-to conversation starters can help learners know where to launch their discourse.

Sentence Starters

Presenting ideas

- I was thinking . . .
- I noticed that . . .
- I justified my reasoning by . . .

Responding to thinking of others

- Could you be more specific about . . .
- I solved it differently by . . .
- I agree/disagree because . . .

Reflecting on understanding

- Now I understand that . . .
- This reminds me of . . .
- Something else I'd like to know is . . .

Scaffolding with questioning strategies

Just as important as knowing how to explain is knowing how to ask questions that provoke a peer to verbalize his thinking. Although NCTM's teaching practices highlight the teacher's responsibility to ask probing questions, students also can assume this responsibility: Students can push one another's thinking far more efficiently by asking questions of their peers than if each must wait for an instructor to come by and ask a pointed question. To promote deep questioning, hark back to the thinking strategies discussed in chapter 3 (see fig. 3.4) and consider how learners might apply those strategies to ignite conversations, as illustrated in figure 5.2.

Thinking strategy	Mathematicians evaluate their own work and the work of others. They . . .	To do this, mathematicians may ask their peers . . .
Ask questions	• clarify why a solution is accurate • consider alternate approaches to the problem-solving process • connect special cases with recognizable patterns	• Why? • Could you think about (or explain) that in another way? • How does ____ relate to what we know about ____?
Determine importance	• ensure that their solution addresses the purpose of the problem • develop an answer that makes sense and is justified with mathematical reasoning • generalize main ideas	• What is it you are trying to solve? • Could you help me understand why that works? • So, what do we need to remember about problems like these?

Fig. 5.2. Mathematicians generate discourse with probing questions.

Thinking strategy	Mathematicians evaluate their own work and the work of others. They . . .	To do this, mathematicians may ask their peers . . .
Draw on background knowledge	• consider whether a solution makes sense, given the context • make connections between related problems and solutions	• What did you already know when you started? • What does this remind you of?
Infer	• deduce the rationale behind a peer's work • analyze a single solution in light of a general principle	• So, you were thinking . . .? • So, this is an example of . . . ?
Model and represent	• develop and refer to models that represent their ideas • understand the thinking of others by examining models • evaluate the effectiveness of various models in a given situation • synthesize and create new models as their understanding evolves	• How could you represent that? • How does your model illustrate your solution? • What is the best way to show this? • How else could we show this?
Monitor for meaning	• assess whether the thinking makes sense • attend to precision • assure clear documentation of solutions	• I still don't understand . . . ; could you explain? • Does that make sense? • How did you record your thinking?
Synthesize	• compare their thinking and work with the work of others • identify commonalities between various solutions to a problem • critique the reasoning behind a solution in light of known principles • contextualize solutions within the landscape of broader principles	• In what ways were our approaches similar? Different? • What did our solutions have in common? • Did you consider . . .? • What would this be an example of?

Fig. 5.2. *Continued*

Capable of both asking and explaining, students are poised to engage in generative discourse. Establishing conversation routines within familiar structures scaffolds a culture of discourse as well. Of the numerous possible conversation structures, select a few to consciously hone in your classroom (see "Conferring" on the next page for ideas). Teach, model, rehearse, and practice those structures. As students become skillful at transitioning into and out of these discussion formats, add to the repertoire. Even if the formats are the same, the conversation will always be different as you introduce new topics.

Offering feedback

Success with any endeavor is enhanced by feedback. After you remind students of the norms and expectations for a given structure, you can then take time to reflect on their adherence

Conferring

The work time of a workshop affords teachers key opportunities to get to know learners as mathematical thinkers. Though your burgeoning email inbox and a pile of papers stacked ready to grade may be calling out to you, remember that the discipline of conferring regularly pays great dividends in generating both mathematical understanding and quality discourse.

To confer is to sit down with an individual or small group, where they are, and ask. It is not about helping or fixing but rather inquiring into their thought patterns and understanding in ways that draw forth articulate thinking. A conferring conversation is best launched with a teacher's open-ended question:

- How's it going?
- What are you thinking?
- Talk to me about . . .

Once students start sharing, probe:

- Say more.
- Help me understand . . .
- Can you explain that in another way?

Several things happen as we confer:

Learners—

- hear us model the language of our inquiry;
- recognize that their ideas and trains of thought are valuable and interesting;
- formulate academic language and explain; and
- increase confidence in their ability to communicate ideas.

Teachers—

- practice teaching as listening;
- get to know students as thinkers;
- understand the backstory of misconception; and
- gather data that helps with future planning.

Conferring takes time. We need not saddle ourselves with the burden of conferring every day but rather can simply set weekly goals of getting around to a handful of students, recording who they are and what we discussed, and going for the next handful the following week. Everyone in earshot benefits. Each time we confer, we are demonstrating the style of conversation learners can emulate when it is their turn to engage in student-to-student discourse.

to those, either by offering feedback yourself or by welcoming learners to self-assess. A simple "How did this go?" invites students to take an honest look at their process: Did we all listen? Contribute? Support one another? Brief reflections of this nature heighten students' self-awareness. And if things head south during discourse, be willing to stop and reset the group midstream so that time is not wasted and culture not corrupted by low-quality conversations. "Whoa! Freeze! This is not what I expected . . . "

Sustaining accountability

When I talk about discourse, some teachers will retort, "What if I ask them to turn and talk about conic sections, and they don't? They talk about basketball or *American Idol*, and it's all just a waste of time." This fear has become reality in too many classrooms, where teachers initiated discourse routines, watched them flop, and returned to lecture-style instruction.

The key to high-quality discourse is accountability. Learners need to know that when you ask them to talk about box-and-whisker plots, you mean it. Start with that: Say it like you mean it. Then hold them accountable. How?

- **Artifacts.** Ask teams to document their conversation in some way.

- **Random calling.** Use Popsicle sticks or a random number generator to select whom to invite to report out; this is a form of warm calling, as discussed earlier.

- **Follow-up work.** Create a need for learners to use the fruits of their conversation to move into the next task.

- **Reflection.** Ask learners to consider their own participation. Did they actively listen? Contribute? Think? Challenge?

More Resources on Discourse

The first and third of these resources are elementary-specific, and the second and last are books for teachers of all content areas, yet each can be helpful to you if read with an open mind.

Choice Words: How Our Language Affects Children's Learning, by Peter Johnston

Classroom Discourse: The Language of Teaching and Learning, by Courtney Cazden

Classroom Discussions: Using Math Talk to Help Students Learn, by Suzanne Chapin, Mary Catherine O'Connor, and Nancy Canavan Anderson

Good Questions for Math Teaching, Grades 5–8: Why Ask Them and What to Ask, by Lainie Schuster and Nancy Anderson

Making Thinking Visible: How to Promote Engagement, Understanding, and Independence for All Learners, by Ron Ritchhart, Mark Church, and Karin Morrison

---

Discourse Structures

A friend of mine, deep in the throes of parenting two toddlers, adopted the experts' recommendation that she get into the habit of offering her young daughters two viable choices at any juncture, thereby avoiding power struggles. She implemented this strategy with such fidelity that one afternoon, her very sincere three-year-old asked, "What would you like to do with us now, Mommy, watch a movie or eat ice cream?" Two choices the preschooler could live with.

This story serves as a reminder that children of all ages are constantly listening, observing, and striving to emulate our discourse patterns. For this reason, as we aspire to inspire top-notch academic talk in the classroom, our words and behavior matter. When we model respect for all ideas—an inquiry stance—and the flexibility to change our own thinking, we demonstrate to students the intellectual character that rigorous discourse demands.

Discourse can take many forms in our classrooms, starting with our small conferring conversations with students, including short, small-group tasks, and extending to include larger debates and discussions.

Little discourse

Brief, succinct intervals for discourse can be integrated into the everyday routine of almost any classroom in the form of paired and small-group conversations, and perhaps including whole-group sharing and discussion. Figure 5.3 offers some structures for engaging learners in these quick conversations, which we might call mini-discourse or "little discourse."

Structure	Purpose	Ideal application	Example
Paired sharing	Articulate understanding	Brief conversations synthesizing learning	"Turn and tell your shoulder partner everything you understand now about similar triangles."
Trios sharing	Brainstorm ideas or possibilities	Short conversations in which multiple viewpoints can further illuminate the complexity of the subject at hand	"Form a trio with two people who do not sit at your table. Together, brainstorm all the ways you might use a cosine to solve a real-world problem."
Homework honing	Compare	Focused discussion of a self-selected problem	"With your partner, choose one problem that was interesting or challenging, and talk about how you approached it. Look for similarities and differences."
Justification conversation	Justify a solution	Gather with peers who agree or disagree with your solution and discuss why	"If you think the solution is 3, go to the front of the room; if you think it is 4, go to the back of the room. There, find a partner and talk about why you think you are correct."

Fig. 5.3. "Little discourse" structures

As with any new routine, discourse structures require explanation and rehearsal to be effective. Let's consider a jiffy workshop (seven minutes in length) in which you might teach the discourse structure of homework honing, as illustrated in figure 5.4.

	Purpose	Teacher voice and role
Mini-lesson (2 mins.)	To prepare students to discuss by explaining the goal	"The purpose of this partnership is not to go over every question on the homework but rather to choose one that you and your partner both found interesting or challenging and to discuss your different approaches— or to brainstorm alternate approaches to the ones you both used. "Just take a moment to select your problem and then share and listen to how each of you solved it. Justify your solutions. This is not about saying, 'I got 42, what did you get?' It might sound like, 'So I was thinking . . .' or 'When I first saw this one . . . ' and you might ask each other to 'say more.'" The teacher-projects those sentence stems on the SMART Board. "You may be called on to present to the group. Questions? "To find your partner, identify someone in the room whose shoes look like yours. Go."
Work time (3 mins.)	For students to pair and discuss	The teacher ensures that everyone is paired up and then confers.
Sharing and reflection (2 mins.)	For learners to give and receive feedback on their writing and synthesize a vision for effective writing.	"I heard Lance and Adam having a really fruitful conversation about different ways to solve number 10, so I am going to ask them to share." The students place their work under the document camera and explain their different approaches to the class. Afterward, the teacher asks, "How did your conversation about this question help you? What do you understand now that you did not know before?"

Fig. 5.4. Jiffy workshop around little discourse, on homework honing

How Should I Group Students?

Group your students however you like; just mix them often and well. Numerous algorithms, systems, structures, and programs are available for matching up learners scientifically, and if you have one that works for you and your class, wonderful. But if you are looking for just the right chemical formula to ensure learning and growth, I recommend entropy. That is how the real world works. We get on a plane, we get a job, we need help jump-starting our car, and whoever turns up is whom we work with. We figure it out. Similarly, I would encourage you to resist the temptation to engineer groups or partners and instead let all learners know that you expect them to work with everyone and that you expect them to work it out. This is a key life lesson.

How Should I Group Students? *continued*

To that end, you might try a variety of systems for random grouping:

- Put names on index cards or Popsicle sticks that you shuffle and match up.

- Use computer programs that assign partners.

- Invite students to team up on the basis of some nonnegotiable quality, such as shirt color or hair length.

- Ask students to line up by birthdate, shoe size, last digit in their phone number, and then match folks up from there.

While entropy is generally my best suggestion, under certain conditions some engineering may be worthwhile. When we have a significant number of English language learners in one class, for example, some key strategies can enhance access:

- Group students of the same home language so that they can process together. Math talk in any language is still math talk.

- Group ELLs with bilingual students who can code switch and support them in comprehending the academic vocabulary.

- Group ELLs with more proficient English speakers who can support them in giving voice to their ideas.

Big discourse

In addition to the opportunities that arise on a daily basis for little discourse, you can create time within math learning experiences for more extended conversation, perhaps still in small groups or on occasions as a whole class. The structures for "big discourse," like those for little discourse, take explanation and rehearsal but, once learned, can create forums for ongoing, engaged conversation about mathematical thinking. Figure 5.5 presents some structures to try.

"That is all I have to say about that," Forrest Gump tells us, but let that not be the case for our math learners. There is always more to say, and each time we invite students to speak their minds, to respond to the ideas of peers, they further articulate their thinking, which deepens their mathematical understanding.

Discourse supports students in developing the disciplinary literacy of mathematicians. Discourse addresses a cornucopia of standards: those for math content and for math practices, as well as for speaking and listening. Most important, high-quality discourse invites learners to engage as thinkers in a social process of figuring things out, a life skill that will serve them well far beyond the confines of our classroom walls.

Turning classroom conversations over to students is an act of courage and an act of hope. When we step aside and trust learners to do the majority of the thinking, discussing, justifying, questioning, and reasoning, we convey to them our great confidence that their good minds are capable and that we teachers are willing to listen, with optimism, to their ideas.

Structure	Purpose	Set up	Process
Carousel discussion: Speak and respond in writing to an artifact	Interpreting	For each table, prepare a different text requiring response: a problem to solve, a piece of student work to examine, etc.	Give each table group a few minutes to read, discuss, and then respond in writing to the text (either on a poster, sticky notes, or a smaller piece of paper). Then rotate the students and invite them to respond to the artifact at the next table, adding to the thinking of the previous group.
Debate: Present differing views on a topic	Persuading with evidence	Select a mathematical issue that can generate controversy, such as lying with statistics, or the importance of understanding ideas vs. knowing algorithms. Invite learners to prepare to speak on one side or another of the issue.	Structure the conversation with time limits and turn-taking, so that no one person or side has a stronger voice. At the conclusion, invite learners to reflect on whether and how their thinking has changed.
Fish bowl: Listen as peers discuss	Hearing multiple perspectives	Offer learners a problem-solving or other task. Arrange students to gather around and silently observe peers at work.	Give observers concrete look-fors: Are they listening for academic language, questioning strategies, collaboration? Debriefing these observations offers a great window into high-quality discourse.
Gallery walk: View and respond to the work of peers	Comparing	Gather learners' work on a task or problem and hang it on the walls throughout the room.	Invite classmates to peruse the work of their peers silently, as in an art gallery, looking for similarities and differences. Discuss.
Peer critique: Listen and respond to work of peers	Comparing	Invite one learner to tell the story of her solution.	Invite students first to listen to their peers present and then to respond with questions, constructive feedback, or comparative statements.
Problem solving: Collaborate to generate a solution	Reasoning	Ask students to work independently first, even for only five minutes, and then to meet with a peer to complete the problem-solving process.	As the student pairs collaborate, remind them that both of them need to document the solution for themselves, agree on it, understand it, and be ready to explain.
Wagon wheels: Brainstorm or discuss ideas	Generating thinking	Gather the class in two standing concentric circles, the inside circle facing out, the outside facing in, so that each student has a partner.	Pose a question to discuss: What are all the ways to make 3? After a minute of time to talk with their partner, invite learners to share. Then get everyone a new partner by spinning the wheel (asking one circle or another to take a given number of steps to the left or right), and ask another question: How is pi useful in the real world?

Fig. 5.5. "Big discourse" structures

93

"Yeah, but . . . "

- *"My students won't talk."*

Sadly, some students fall silent during their years in school. But silence can be boring and lonely and can limit one's engagement and learning, so we had best not let them stay there. Start with easy topics: a comic to respond to, a conversation about lunch or sports. Teacher Kathy Sampson had a stuffed ostrich she would toss onto a student's desk: If it landed on yours, that meant that at some point during that class period, you had to make a comment. Students played along and soon were saying a whole lot more.

Affirm participation; practice discourse structures, and build from there.

- *"When I ask students to share, they just go off . . . "*

Ask a targeted question. Keep the talk time short. Follow up by holding students accountable, "Azalea, what did you and your partner say about the pattern in number 3?" If they shrug, smile and wait. Pretty soon, they will know you mean business.

- ***"The kids in my class are so rude and mean to each other, I cannot ask them to respond to their peers' thinking."***

Ouch. Tragically, the culture of school can erode into *Lord of the Flies* if we are not vigilant about our expectations for human excellence. Start a conversation about how you like to be treated when you share your ideas. Invite students to respond. Through discussion, build their social imagination, their ability to envision a circumstance from the perspective of another. Set norms. Stick with them. When transgressions occur, talk about feelings.

- ***"I've really tried hard to get my students to speak like mathematicians and collaborate together. But they just don't seem to be able to express their ideas effectively."***

Start where they are. Offer scaffolds and sentence stems, accessible topics and explicit vocabulary instruction. Notice and name what they are doing well. Write down the smart things you hear them say, and post those quotes, each attributed to its speaker, around the room. No one was born knowing how to tie shoes, and eventually we all learned. So it is with discourse: With devotion, support, and persistence, all things are possible.

 **Discourse Planning Template**

Writing as Mathematicians

Writing is thinking. To write well is to think clearly. That's why it's so hard.

—David McCullough, interview, 2002

Problems of the Day

- Why write in math?

- How can we effectively integrate writing instruction into math workshops?

Algebra 2 student Kavya wrote about her statistical analysis of women's Olympic ski jump scores:

After analyzing the data and multiple visual representations of the Women's Normal Hill Individual Ski Jump from the 2014 Sochi Winter Olympics, it can be determined that the participant's performance depended on the situation. Women's Normal Hill Individual is a Winter Olympic event where thirty women from all around the world competed by skiing and eventually jumping off a high ramp. This event was recently added this year and thus, I was interested to see women finally show off their skills in an event like this. Ski jump winners are determined by points. Points are awarded based on distance, an automatic sixty points if the participant reaches the "critical point" and additional points either added or subtracted accordingly depending on if the skier goes over the critical point or comes up short. Style points are also awarded by a team of five judges based on flight, landing, and outrun. Any extra points are added or deducted based off the gate rule and a wind factor.

Statistics from both the first and final round show that the thirty female participants' performance decreased from the first round to the final round. Percent change calculated with the mean shows there was a 2.34% decrease from the first to the final round. This means that the average score decreased from one round to the other. In addition, although the maximum score in both rounds did not change much (only a 0.8 difference), the minimum score dropped from 73.3 to 42.4. This 30.9 point difference and the fact that 42.4 is an outlier in the lower range proves that there was a drastic drop in scores, especially in the lower scoring participants of the first round. Also, the IQR (interquartile range) shows a difference of 2.9 from the first round to the final round, but the range has a huge difference of 30.1 points, from 53.5 (first round) to 83.6 (final round) This makes the point that the **average** performing participants didn't vary too much from the first round to the final round, but as a whole, the participants' scores became way more spread out, especially in the lower quartile. As seen on the box-and-whisker plot, the "whisker" connecting the minimum to Q1 is larger for the final round compared to the first round. Also, the standard deviation for the first round is 11.16 points while it is 15.18 points for the final round. Therefore, more spread out scores mean people were scoring in the extreme lows thus, proving that the participants, especially the low performing individuals' performance depends on the situation. A higher range means scores are not very condensed in an area again, proving that performance decreased from the first round to the final round.

Scaffolded by teacher Tracey Shaw's careful planning, Kavya and her classmates documented their mathematical understanding in an in-depth writing project that included tables, graphs, and data displays, as well as expository pieces like the one above. This large writing project, which will be further detailed later in the chapter, is but one example of the ways in which teachers can engage learners in writing as mathematicians, with tasks large and small.

Why Teach Writing in Math?

Many secondary teachers I have worked with had developed habits of skipping over questions in their math curricula that invited narrative response for two simple reasons: (1) students didn't want to write, and (2) teachers didn't want to read what students wrote. So, why should we bother integrating writing into math courses?

Writing improves students' thinking and problem solving

A meta-analysis of research on the relationship between writing and mathematics achievement assembled by Pugalee and colleagues (2004, p. 27) yielded an important finding:

> Students who wrote descriptions of their thinking were significantly more successful in the problem solving tasks than students who verbalized their thinking. Differences in metacognitive behaviors also support the premise that writing can be an effective tool in supporting metacognitive behaviors.

Other research indicates that math learners who complete fewer problems but devote time to composing explanations actually learn and understand more than students who simply crank through page upon page of calculations (Senk and Thompson 2003). NCTM's Mathematics Teaching Practices suggest that we "use and connect mathematical representations" (2014). Writing is one such representation.

Demonstrating mathematical knowledge requires writing

Half of the math section of the 2013 National Assessment of Educational Progress (NAEP) contained multiple-choice questions, while the other half required constructed written responses. The NAEP is but one of the many standardized tests learners may be expected to complete in their school years, yet increasingly these exams include significant constructed-response segments where students need to articulate their mathematical thinking in writing.

When we ask learners to put their ideas on paper, we provide an opportunity for them to synthesize their thoughts and cement their understanding. NCTM's Mathematics Teaching

Practices encourage us to "elicit and use evidence of student thinking." An invitation for students to write is an opportunity to do just that.

Further, the Common Core Standards for Mathematical Practice invite learners to reason and argue, which can include both discourse and writing. By integrating regular writing routines into our math workshops, we welcome learners to see themselves as constructors of knowledge, capable of providing their own claims, explanations, and critiques as mathematicians.

As they did for reading, the authors of the Common Core developed specific standards for writing to be integrated within learners' experiences in history/social studies, science, and technical subjects (see fig. 6.1). Take a moment to read and annotate these, noting which you believe are most relevant and useful for math learners. This list includes all ten Common Core anchor standards for writing, but note that the science and technical subjects literacy standards do not expect or require science and math teachers to teach or use narrative writing with their students. Rather, they are expected to emphasize teaching and using argument (W.1) and informative/explanatory writing (W.2).

Text Types and Purposes

- Write arguments to support claims in an analysis of substantive topics or texts using valid reasoning and relevant and sufficient evidence. (W.1)

- Write informative/explanatory texts to examine and convey complex ideas and information clearly and accurately through the effective selection, organization, and analysis of content. (W.2)

- Write narratives to develop real or imagined experiences or events using effective technique, well-chosen details, and well-structured event sequences. (W.3)

Production and Distribution of Writing

- Produce clear and coherent writing in which the development, organization, and style are appropriate to task, purpose, and audience. (W.4)

- Develop and strengthen writing as needed by planning, revising, editing, rewriting, or trying a new approach. (W.5)

- Use technology, including the Internet, to produce and publish writing and to interact and collaborate with others. (W.6)

Research to Build and Present Knowledge

- Conduct short as well as more sustained research projects based on focused questions, demonstrating understanding of the subject under investigation. (W.7)

- Gather relevant information from multiple print and digital sources, assess the credibility and accuracy of each source, and integrate the information while avoiding plagiarism. (W.8)

- Draw evidence from literary or informational texts to support analysis, reflection, and research. (W.9)

Range of Writing

- Write routinely over extended time frames (time for research, reflection, and revision) and shorter time frames (a single sitting or a day or two) for a range of tasks, purposes, and audiences. (W.10)

Fig. 6.1. Common Core State Standards: College and Career Readiness Anchor Standards for Writing (CCSSI 2010)

Which sorts of writing seem important for your students to know and be able to accomplish in the context of their math learning? What will you leave for your colleagues across the hall?

Writing instruction need not be a tangent that takes away from math learning time or interferes with learners' mathematical growth. Rather, it can be integrated into regular classwork with a few more minutes here and there intentionally devoted to explicit instruction, critique, and reflection. You may be among the many math teachers who already integrate a good ration of student writing into their classes, which is wonderful. National writing expert Penny Kittle raises a concern: "In too many classrooms, we assign and assess writing without teaching the craft of it" (2014, p. 34).

In this chapter, we will explore how you, as a math teacher, can offer specific, helpful writing instruction tailored to the sorts of writing tasks that promote mathematical thinking and understanding.

Pre-writing

Writing begins with knowing what you want to say. This is why the discourse chapter precedes the writing chapter in this book: Discourse provides learners with opportunities for oral rehearsal before they begin to pencil a sentence. Although some students may come to the craft of writing with great enthusiasm and creativity, others clam up at the thought of composing their own thoughts in this form. For this reason, all learners—and especially English language learners—benefit greatly from varied chances to gather thoughts, generate ideas, test-drive arguments, sketch relationships, or otherwise prime the pump of their thinking before being expected to write even a sentence.

Especially early in the school year, as you are establishing writing routines in your class (whether assigning small tasks or major projects), a few minutes devoted to "pre-writing" can greatly enhance learners' productivity during their writing time. Pre-writing can include—

• individual, independent think time;

• paired or small-group conversations in response to specific prompts;

• pencil-and-paper tasks, including outlining ideas, completing graphic organizers, or sketching mind maps (see fig. 6.2).

In addition to pre-writing, models of effective writing can also serve to spur students on in their work. Even seeing one parallel example of what the task is "supposed to look like" can effectively motivate a learner to begin.

What Writing Advances and Demonstrates Mathematical Understanding?

In the context of math class, we can engage students in two kinds of writing: "little writing"—tasks that span just a few minutes—and "big writing"—tasks that include numerous iterations and culminate in polished products. Little writing tasks can include

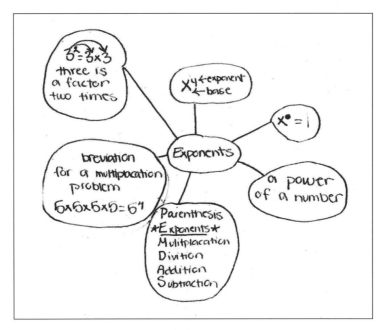

Fig. 6.2. A student's mind map for exponents

low-stakes, quick-response prompts peppered throughout each week; some teachers refer to these sorts of tasks as "writing to learn." Typically these are ungraded, though often handed in. Big writing tasks include in-depth, math-related writing projects and require a significant investment of instruction and support; these are typically integrated less often across each semester or year.

Little Writing

Short, friendly writing on a regular basis has a big place within each student's math learning experience, as described by the tenth Common Core writing standard. This little writing might include "prompt writing" of the sort most often found on standardized tests—justifying a solution or explaining a concept—yet our repertoire of brief writing tasks can also be expanded to include some of the suggestions in figure 6.3.

Often by the time students have reached secondary school, they have developed bad habits of believing that a fragment of vague description will suffice in response to a math writing prompt, and they respond with no more than "Because I minused 42 from 98," "That's what the question was asking me," or even "I don't know." Without vision and inter-vention, the ability of these learners to write as mathematicians is unlikely to grow. In teach-ing students to respond thoughtfully to small writing tasks, we can embrace a miniature version of a workshop, lasting perhaps only seven minutes at a time, as detailed in figure 6.4.

In the context of your instruction, it may not be realistic to devote seven minutes each day to such a routine. Yet, if you spend time even once a week affirming your expectations for writing and asking learners to reflect on the strengths of their work, your investment can rapidly ratchet up the quality of the students' writing. That, in turn, can deepen the quality of learners' mathematical understanding, which is your ultimate goal.

Task	Key features	Sample prompt
Explain a concept	• Describes general idea and relevance of concept • Offers one or more specific examples • May include words, pictures, equations	What is a sine?
Summarize a process	• Articulates goal • Details procedure, step by step • Shows calculations • May include illustrations	How did you calculate the height of the flagpole?
Justify a solution	• Explains mathematical concept or principle being applied • Describes problem • Articulates process of solving, including all calculations	Why is your solution reasonable?
Critique a solution	• States agreement or disagreement • Gives specific evidence • Connects evidence with reasoning	Is Beth right?
Reflect on content	• Explains what learner understands • Asks questions about areas of confusion	What do you know now about how trigonometry can be used to solve real-world problems?
Reflect on process	• Critiques success • Articulates transferrable learning	What did you learn about yourself as a mathematician?

Fig. 6.3. "Little writing" task ideas

Parallel Examples

If students are about to be asked to justify that 3 cubed is 27, we undermine their opportunity for original thought if we use that very prompt as the example in our mini-lesson. Rather, we can conjure up a parallel, simpler, illustration, such as 1 squared is 1. This example is called "parallel" because the thinking process required is aligned with the work we are about to request of learners, but by demonstrating with this example, rather than the task they are about to do, we do not steal their chance to think.

Sentence stems to launch writing

Figure 6.5 shows how specific questions prompted a high-quality student reflection. Similarly, some teachers offer sentence stems to support students' writing. These can be particularly effective when inaugurating a ritual and routine of writing early in the year, but they might be considered a scaffold to remove across time as learners' independence as writers grows. Many books on writing or discourse offer lists of open-ended stems; figure 6.6 includes just a few favorites.

Little writing of this sort can be useful during reflection at the end of a workshop or as an exit ticket during the reflection component of a workshop, and it can also be integrated

	Purpose	Teacher Voice
Mini-lesson (2 mins.)	Prepare students to write by offering specific instruction and parallel examples (see "Parallel Examples" on the preceding page).	"Question 12 asks you to justify your solution. Think about that for a moment. What does 'justify' mean? *Justification* includes giving the reasons behind your thinking, defending your solution. "So, if I want to justify that 1 squared is 1, I might explain that as follows: Squaring a number means multiplying it times itself; 1 is a factor two times. So, 1 squared means 1 times 1, which is 1. "What do you notice about my justification?" [*The teacher affirms students when they note that her justification explained the mathematical concept in general and then describes that principle in the context of this problem in particular.*]
Work time (2 mins.)	Students write.	[*Silent work time*]
Sharing and reflection (2 mins.)	Learners give and receive feedback on their writing, synthesize a vision for effective writing.	"Please turn to your shoulder partner and share your justification; your partner's job is to listen and offer feedback. Did you describe the mathematical principle you were applying? Did you describe this specific problem in light of that? Then your partner can respond with one thing she appreciates about your writing, as well as one suggestion for improvement." [*To the whole group after the partner sharing is complete:*] "Would anyone like to share what a partner wrote and what was helpful about it?" "So, what does it mean to *justify*? What are the ingredients in a high-quality justification?"

Fig. 6.4. A jiffy math-writing workshop

throughout learners' work time, following a mini-lesson, or during work time. There is no "right time" to ask students to stop and write. It is always the write/right time!

Exit tickets are one common, quick writing task that many math teachers employ as a closing to their daily lessons, a written check-in for students to complete on the way out the door. Your exit ticket might be a problem to solve, a question to answer, or a concept to summarize. Once you ask students to write exit tickets or any other little piece of math writing, take time to read their thoughts, even if only glancing over their shoulders as they write. I often sort students' exit tickets into stacks with common themes or needs: These students understand the purpose of PEMDAS; these students do not yet. Once I have their responses sorted, I can make a plan for how I will support their various needs during our very next workshop. In this way, student writing can offer valuable feedback on our instruction.

Math notebooks

Little writing can be completed anywhere—in margins, on sticky notes, on the back side of a handout, at the bottom of a page of worked problems. Yet many math teachers find that the specific routine of a math notebook works well as a friendly home for their students' regular math writing, as modeled in figure 6.7.

Fig. 6.5. Student reflection

Purpose	Sentence stem ideas
Explain a concept	• The big idea of _____ is . . . • _____ is important because . . .
Summarize a process	• I started out by . . . • First . . . Second . . . • In order to . . .
Justify a solution	• I am confident in my solution because . . . • I chose to solve in this way because . . . • I would like to know more about . . .
Critique a solution	• I agree (or disagree) because . . . • I am wondering . . . • What if . . .
Reflect on content	• I understand . . . • What I learned today about . . . • I need to remember . . .
Reflect on process	• What helped me most . . . • My greatest challenge . . . • I used to think . . . and now I think . . . and so I will . . .

Fig. 6.6. Some sentence stem ideas

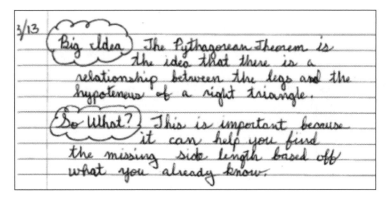

Fig. 6.7. From a student's math notebook

Math notebooks can be anything from store-bought, graph-paper-filled composition books to a sheaf of papers stapled together. The big idea of a math notebook is that it serves as a ready place to log thinking and understanding. These notebooks can be home to vocabulary, problems solved, articles read, discourse notes, and reflections, as well as the variety of little writing tasks described in this chapter.

Eighth-grade teacher Deb Maruyama builds a strong ritual of math notebook writing across the year. She trains students to set their notebook pages up in a specific format not much different from that used by naturalists to record field notes. Deb asks students to pause in their work regularly to record thinking by writing—

- a summary;

- an "Aha!"—something new that the student now understands; or

- a "Yeah, but . . . ?"— a question.

Students readily respond to this routine, carrying their notebooks with them at all times throughout Deb's math workshops. "At the beginning of the year," Deb says, "when I ask them to write for two minutes, they whine and complain, 'I don't know what to say!' but by the end of the year, when I give them eight minutes to write, and students are like, 'Hey! Miss! That's not enough time'" (Maruyama 2014). This is because Deb devotes time to training math learners as writers: She models how to complete writing tasks, offers learners feedback on their writing at regular intervals, and builds their stamina across time.

Now, some of you have already done the math: 30 students times 5 periods equals 150 notebooks. Hence the question, When and how am I going to read all those? Here are some strategies math teachers use to respond to students' little writing in a timely manner:

- Know your purpose and be realistic. Why are you reading these, and what are you looking for?

- Avoid using your own time to account for assignments completed or compliance with formatting requirements, and instead devote your energy to responding to learners' thinking.

- Make a weekly schedule and stick to it. Commit to reading one class's notebooks each day, or five students' from each class each day, or some other target. Read the notebooks in the classroom during your planning time, so you are not burdened with carrying them around or schlepping them home.

- Keep track. Log which notebooks you see when, both as an accounting strategy and as an affirmation of your own effort.

- Give feedback. Students need to know that you are reading their work. Feedback might include individual responses in the form of comments, stamps, stickers, or sketches, collective responses presented as global feedback to the class, or generic individual responses. Be creative. One teacher who found herself writing the same comment in notebook after notebook printed out a page of labels with that feedback and then could apply those as needed.

- Let learners respond to one another's notebooks. Students don't always need to hear from you about their writing and thinking, but they do need to hear from someone. If you ask learners to write, ensure that you do something with that writing, indicating to all that their work matters.

Notebooking requires an investment of time and energy, both by learners and teachers, yet can be a powerful routine to reinforce the value of writing to learn mathematics.

What Do Professional Mathematicians Write About?

Within all the proofs, treatises, and exposés written by mathematicians across the ages, mathematicians have consistently written to think through or reflect on the following:

- Observations of mathematical relationships
- Questions related to mathematical phenomena or problems
- Accounts of how they solved a problem
- Logical arguments and proofs
- Expositions of background
- Explanations of why they think they are right
- Explanations of why they think someone else is wrong

How might students in your classroom engage in similar writing projects?

Big Writing

Little writing will most likely comprise the bulk of the written work you ask your fledgling mathematicians to do each year and, if assembled, would weigh in with a significant word count. There is also a place in our math instruction—perhaps just once a semester, to begin— for "big writing": long-term, in-depth written tasks that involve more significant dedication of instructional time and that culminate in rich products showcasing student understanding. Glance at figure 6.8 and consider the sorts of writing that mathematicians have historically engaged in. The list includes ideas for both argument and narrative writing, as suggested by the Common Core. Most likely, you can envision a wide array of potential writing projects for your students that would both require and build their disciplinary literacy skills.

Task	Key features	Sample prompt
Argument and opinion writing (W.1)		
General	• Responds to a question or issue • Includes a claim, evidence (data), and supporting reasoning • May include counterclaims and rebuttals	What is the relationship between infant mortality and life expectancy in nations around the world?
Proof	• Is a specific form of argument • Includes mathematical axioms, definitions, and theorems as evidence • Has a formal, logical structure	Was Pythagoras right?
Critique	• Responds to the ideas or solutions of others • States an opinion and supports it with specific evidence. • Can include and justify an alternate claim or solution	From a mathematical standpoint, is the electoral college fair? Why or why not?
Expository writing (W.2)		
Explanation	• Describes a concept or idea • May include diagrams, words, and pictures • Contextualizes concept, describes utility and relevance	What does it mean to divide fractions?
Research	• Synthesizes information from multiple sources • Is free of opinion or analysis	Where did pi come from?
Reflection	• Describes an experience in first person • Offers specific examples supported with analysis • Applies learning to next context	How have you grown as a mathematician this year?

Fig. 6.8. "Big writing" ideas

Scaffolding Extended Writing Projects in Math

Many math teachers who have experimented with integrating writing projects into their courses find that it is easy to assign long-term writing projects but tough to get high-quality results from students. To catalyze learners' investment in and completion of worthy written work, we math teachers can look to our language arts colleagues for ideas. Genre study, the writing process, and writers' workshops are three specific, transferrable practices that can yield great results in terms of learners' engagement and achievement as mathematical writers.

Genre study

Genre study is a practice that introduces learners to a specific writing style through numerous examples, invites students to notice and wonder about that genre's style, and then asks them to write "under the influence" of that genre. Educator Katie Wood Ray describes a genre study: "Framing instruction as study represents an essential stance to teaching and learning, an *inquiry* stance, characterized by repositioning curriculum as the outcome of instruction rather than the starting point" (2006, p. 19).

Genre study entrusts to students the responsibility of figuring out, as writers, how their work ought to look and sound by examining parallel examples, sparing students the experience of writing as an over-scaffolded, paint-by-numbers exercise or a blind guess-and-check activity. Through genre studies, learners gain an understanding of what quality looks like. As discussed in chapter 3, understanding a genre deeply allows us to become more careful readers of that genre, and, as Ray points out, genre studies also enhance learners' writing.

In her popular text *Study Driven* (2006), Katie Wood Ray describes five steps for effective genre study, presented in figure 6.9.

Stage	Description	Math example
Gathering text	Teachers and students collect samples or "mentor texts" of the genre.	I gather a number of proofs to share, including the work of former students, as well as professional mathematicians.
Setting the stage	Students understand that they will be writing in the genre of the study.	I describe the role of mathematical proofs and explain that by writing, these learners are joining the ranks of true mathematicians.
Immersion	Students and teachers pore over the gathered texts and make observations about their structure, format, and style, drawing inferences about the process that the writer engaged in to produce each piece.	I spread copies of five or six different proofs at each table for learners to peruse during work time.
Close study	Students and teachers develop a shared description of the key elements of the genre, perhaps listing it on a poster to refer to and revise.	After time for small-group conversation, we gather and list the key elements of a proof: logic, argument, reasoning . . .
Writing under the influence	Students engage in a writing project in the manner of the genre studied.	With support, learners write their first proofs about the angles of a triangle.

Fig. 6.9. Genre study. Based on Ray (2006).

Mentor Texts

The purpose of genre study is to present learners with a variety of examples of the genre at hand. Throughout the writing process, time devoted to further analysis of mentor texts—exemplars from the genre—can galvanize students' understanding of how their product might look. Analyzing a mentor text could be the focus of a mini-lesson or a way to introduce the rubric: Ask learners to assess a sample or mentor text, using the rubric as a tool. Carefully select (or create) mentor texts that illustrate the exact qualities you hope students will emulate in their writing. Discussions of exemplars can be far more helpful than rubrics in developing learners' understanding of your expectations.

As the example in the figure illustrates, by teaching the "genre" of mathematical proofs, you are spared the task of explaining each step of proof writing, and students gain the benefit of viewing multiple models. And because they have authored the descriptors of quality, students also feel compelled to aspire to the vision and complete a top-notch proof.

Writing as a process

Once students, through a genre study, gain a vision of what they aspire to write, a number of additional scaffolds within the writing process can support their progress: modeling, graphic organizers, multiple drafts, and peer critiques. Writing is not linear; it is messy, iterative. This chapter alone had six drafts. As a math teacher, I was never trained in the writing process or how to facilitate it, either for myself or for my students. Yet, once learned, this process has supported my growth as a writer and my students' as well. When doing big writing, learners benefit from the gift of time as well as the support of strategies to move their early thinking to a complete piece that effectively communicates mathematical reasoning and argument, as described by the Common Core.

Modeling

One of the most powerful inspirations for student writing is modeling—not simply showing them completed mentor texts, but actually modeling the process of writing and the thinking behind it. Picture this: You at the front of the room, writing under the document camera or on the interactive whiteboard, starting your own piece in the genre: "So I am thinking about my claim, and I am pretty sure I want to argue that global warming is not a problem. When I look at the data on climate trends over the past one million years, I see that earth has gone through cycles of heating and cooling. I am going to use those data to claim that global warming is normal and natural. I need more evidence, though. I wonder where else I should look?"

By thinking aloud in this way, you illustrate for students how a writer of an argument thinks herself into a position based on evidence. Thinking aloud is not about making up fictional stories about what you imagine it might be like to write. Rather, it is actually revealing the authentic inner workings of your mind as you plan or compose in real time, with students watching. Let them see your own disciplinary literacy in action as you write mathematical text and do the hard work of problem solving and reasoning something through as you write.

Graphic organizers

Graphic organizers can serve as another helpful scaffold to support students in planning and executing extended writing projects. These can be developed directly out of the genre study to include all the appropriate elements of the piece. Learners might first use a graphic organizer to dissect a mentor text, noticing and naming the components, and then use it as a planner for their own piece. Many templates are available online, yet the best are those that you and your students create yourselves because they will be tailored to the genre and the task.

Completing a graphic organizer is a wonderful prewriting technique that helps get learners' ideas out before they are facing a blank page or screen. Figure 6.10 is one such organizer, created by Annie Patterson, to scaffold learners' planning of written arguments.

Claim: What do you think? (Answer the question.)			
Evidence: Why do you think that? (Cite expert opinion, research, statistics, quotes, data, analysis, surveys . . .)			
Reasoning: How does your evidence support your claim? (Connect your claim and evidence.)			
Conclusion: What should be done? (Summarize, suggest consequences, call to action)			

Fig. 6.10. Planning for writing argument. Created by Annie Patterson; used with permission.

Drafting

Writing to learn and other little writing tasks typically are not revisited or rewritten; big writing projects invite multiple drafts and revision in light of feedback. This process of composing, reviewing, and rewriting is known as *drafting*. At the launch of a project, let students know your expectations for how they will work through the task. How many drafts should they plan to complete? What should happen in between drafts? Does the piece need to be typed, and if so, at what stage? Are learners expected to hand in all drafts and rubrics to illustrate the process, or just a final product?

Often teachers ask students to share their early drafts with peers, revise those based on the rubric and classmates' input, and then present later drafts to the teacher. This can enhance efficiency of assessment, as well as motivate learners to own their own definitions of quality.

Peer critique

As students progress through the stages of writing projects, we can support their progress with structured peer critiques. Within the context of your math workshops, you have most likely already cultivated a community of learners capable of offering critical, kind feedback in ways that promote thinking. The same peer support is necessary for learners as they strive to move their math writing forward. Establish the expectation that, as an editorial team, learners act as allies and serve as resources to one another, offering specific, helpful, respectful feedback on their pieces.

We can encourage students' compassionate comments with structures for giving feedback, which might include—

- warm feedback only (noting only what you appreciated);

- comments and questions (remembering that comments need to be constructive);

- "plus-delta" (noting one thing you liked and one thing you might suggest revising);

- believing and doubting game (sharing areas that you agree with [believe] and areas that need more evidence or support [doubting]).

108

Structures for peer feedback may include—

- paired sharing (partners trade papers and offer each other feedback);

- editorial groups (small groups receive copies of one another's papers to read and then discuss collectively one at time);

- author's chair (one author reads her work aloud to the class and receives comments).

Writing about Statistics: The Reporter Project

High school teacher Tracey Shaw and her colleagues engage Algebra 2 learners in a significant writing project each year: the Reporter Project. In the unit on probability and statistics, each student selects a competition—perhaps an Olympic event, a high school sport, or a Rubik's cube race—and compares data about that event from one year to the next. The goal of the project is for students to deepen their understanding of how mathematicians, statisticians, economists, and other professionals use statistics to make an argument or defend a stance, as well as how they can mislead us with statistics. Within this project, learners build on their understanding of mean, median, mode, and average, as well as box-and-whisker plots, and then learn the concepts of standard deviation and normal distribution.

Tracey launches the project at the beginning of the second semester by modeling a data analysis task all her own: She presents the exam scores of each of her Algebra 2 classes from the end of the first semester and asks, "Who did better on the final? What information would you use to defend the proposition that the other class did better [counterargument]?" This conversation heats up; soon she introduces the double box-and-whisker plot and further engages learners in a discussion of what "better" means.

Learners' first tasks as they start the project are to develop a proposal describing which sport they want to study, why, and which data they will use. Students have the option to explore one of the following questions:

• Does how participants perform depend on the situation? (comparing rounds of a competition)

• Have participants gotten better over time (for example, 1980 vs. 2014)?

In making decisions about which sport and which data to study, learners realize that not all sports lend themselves to these questions, and that they need particular data, with limited variables, to address these questions well.

Once their proposal is approved, learners launch into analyzing their data every way they can, using all the methods of statistical representation they know: stem-and-leaf, box-and-whisker, and more. Development of these graphic representations is easily supported within the context of the statistics unit.

The next challenge is the written analysis. To scaffold this, Tracey relies on a genre study and the writing process. In analyzing mentor texts, students look for claims, evidence, reasoning, and inferences, pulling apart arguments to

Writing about Statistics: The Reporter Project, *continued*

understand their DNA. Students spend time studying both strong and weak examples to develop their own definitions of an effective one. Students read and annotate several sample texts, examining the content of each paragraph, and then use those as models to compose their own analyses.

Once their first drafts are completed, Tracey's students give feedback to one another, both positive comments and suggestions for improvement. Each student mounts the final draft of his written analysis, along with all of his hand-drawn data displays, on a poster to share with the class. A quick look through the stack of posters shows top-quality work, both in data analysis and written arguments.

Teaching Writing in a Math Workshop

Although the writing process can span a number of days or weeks, writer's workshop is that daily cycle of learning, composing, and reflecting that takes place within the confines of a class period. As described in chapter 2, a workshop is an ideal forum to promote learners' own thinking and understanding. In fact, the notion of workshop-model instruction developed in Donald Graves's (1983) writing classroom research and has been adapted for apprenticing readers, scientists, mathematicians, and others. Whether teaching writing or math or some combination of the two, we can use workshop structure as a means to support learners' agency and understanding.

A daily writing workshop may be devoted to any one of the writing process activities described above: analyzing mentor texts, modeling writing, working with graphic organizers, drafting, or engaging in peer critique.

For example, if your writing workshop on a particular day is focused on peer critique, your mini-lesson will introduce learners to the purpose and structure of the task. The bulk of the work time will be devoted to engaging in the critique itself, and the reflection time will serve as an opportunity for learners to recognize how this conversation was helpful to them as writers and mathematicians. This is but one example; from here you can envision creating writing workshops that feature large chunks of time for learners to grow as writers about mathematics, with the support of instruction during the mini-lesson and conferring during the work time. Refer to chapter 2 for more insight on the flow of a workshop.

Assessing big writing

If we listen to author Steven Covey, we know how critical it is for all of us to begin with the end in mind. Thus, we help students meet high standards when we provide them with specific descriptors of quality in the form of a rubric at the outset of the project. There are a lot of crummy ones out there detailing the number of errors that students need to make to lose a given number of points. Instead, I recommend developing and presenting learners with *additive rubrics*—rubrics that detail in positive language all that you *do* want students to do. Additive rubrics build from a description of basic competence (in a column on the left) to progressively describe proficient work. These student-friendly rubrics support learners in perceiving themselves and their work positively. Figure 6.11 offers one example of an additive rubric for argument writing.

		1	2	3	4	Score/ Comments
			All of 1, plus . . .	All of 2, plus . . .	All of 3, plus . . .	
Content	Claim		States claim.	Claim is clear and related to topic.	Claim makes clear argument in academic language.	
	Evidence	Includes data.	Presents factual evidence.	Evidence provided is factual and connects to claim.	Ample evidence is provided to support claim.	
	Reasoning		Reasoning is present.	Reasoning connects evidence to claim.	Reasoning is clear and convincing.	
Vocabulary			Some technical vocabulary is used.	Most of the expected content-related vocabulary is used.	Accurate academic vocabulary is used throughout.	
Structure		Includes sections appropriate to the content.	Organized. Formal style. Title and subtitles (if applicable).	Paragraphs include introductory sentences. Clear introduction, body, and conclusion.	Flows logically throughout.	
Mechanics		Is written.	Is comprehensible.	Is free from errors that obscure meaning.	Is publication ready.	
Comments:					Total	

Developed in collaboration with members of the North Feeder System Math/Science Writing Cohort, 2013–14. © PEBC, used with permission.

Fig. 6.11. A rubric for writing math argument

When it comes to grading, you serve students best by focusing on one aspect of their writing at a time, determined by their needs and strengths. Do not feel obliged to mark every error with a red pen. The red ink only alarms and intimidates students and, in fact, has been shown by research to be completely ineffectual (Daniels, Zemelman, and Steineke 2007). Instead, set a goal as you begin reading each paper. What are you looking for: a cohesive argument? clear logic? Think substance, not mechanics. Devote your eye to finding evidence of the learners' proficiency or needs along those lines.

Make a few marks within the text, but focus on leaving the authors with a specific feedback sandwich: one thing they did well, one or two aspects to work on, and a final accolade. In this way, you will spur them on with clear direction for revision in the next draft: "Adam, your writing is so clear that I could follow your thinking through each step of the proof. As you revise, please include accurate calculations to back up your claims. Congratulations on expressing your mathematical thinking with such clarity!"

Write On

Writing is an opportunity to hone thinking. When we invite learners to pause in their work to engage in quick, brief writing tasks, or on occasion to write a long treatise as a mathematician, we support them in synthesizing their understanding, sharpening their communication skills, and developing the confidence to express ideas. Although writing instruction has not traditionally been the purview of math teachers, writing has always been part and parcel of the work of mathematicians.

Writing is a response to NCTM's Mathematics Teaching Practices, inviting us to explore multiple representations with learners. Writing is a means to access the Common Core Standards for Mathematical Practice related to reasoning and justification. And writing is a path to students' mathematical understanding, and well worth the investment of students' learning time.

"Yeah, but . . . "

- *"Where can I find good mentor texts for math writing?"*

The writing of professional mathematicians is always a good starting place for mentor texts, and many good texts can now be found online. Look to the work of Archimedes, Einstein, Euclid, Feynman, Newton, Pascal, and Pythagoras, for a start. Another great strategy is to use other students' writing as mentor texts. Save the best pieces from this year, take the names off, and present those to next year's class as examples. Under some circumstances, you may need to create the mentor text yourself, which is actually a good way to climb inside the task and truly understand what it takes to write that sort of piece, better equipping you to support students as they begin.

- *"You lost me way back there. I have no time for this."*

It can be very difficult to envision adding one more thing to your job description as a busy math teacher. If you can come to think of writing as part of the math learning process rather than as a task separate and distinct from it, that may help. Integrating writing is not about adding more to your weekly schedule but about working smarter. Research suggests that reflection is more beneficial than rote practice. Might you be able to sacrifice some skills practice time for a writing-to-learn task? When it comes to big writing, consider saving this project for a strategic time of year: between Thanksgiving and winter break, or toward the end of school when learners are ready for a change of pace. This project need not take over your life for weeks on end, but it may require sacrificing some other activities. What are you willing to let go of to integrate writing?

- *"I decided to teach math because I did not want to have to waste a lot of time grading."*

Assessing writing does take more time than assessing a page of numeric responses. Here are some ideas on how to grade big writing projects efficiently:

- o Give students the rubric up front, have them self-assess and revise their first draft, and then invite a peer to assess their second draft before they revise again. Don't collect anything until the third draft.

- o Have a grading party. Invite friends and colleagues to spend an evening together reading and responding to students' work in relation to a rubric.

- o Pace yourself. If you know you have a big stack of papers coming in, plan ahead for the time it will require. Writing is thinking, and our learners' thinking merits the courtesy of our reply.

Now What?

Far better it is to dare mighty things, to win glorious triumphs, even though checked by failure, than to take rank with those poor spirits who neither enjoy much nor suffer much, because they live in the gray twilight that knows neither victory nor defeat.

—Theodore Roosevelt, *The Strenuous Life: Essays and Addresses*

Problems of the Day

- How am I going to fit all this in?

- Where shall I begin?

The purpose of teaching, of education, is understanding. My hope is that as you have spent time with this book, you have come to understand a few important points:

- Literacy education is the responsibility of a civilized nation to its youth.

- Mathematical understanding is intimately linked to literacy.

- Math teachers can integrate high-quality literacy instruction without sacrificing students' content understanding; in fact, literacy and mathematical achievement are symbiotic.

So how might one begin?

Appreciate Interconnectedness

A few math teachers whom I meet initially respond to the idea of integrating literacy with a sigh and a prayer that this school or districtwide initiative, like others, will pass away without causing them to change what they are already comfortable doing in their own classrooms. Yet those who linger and are willing to experiment with threading explicit reading, vocabulary, discourse, and writing instruction through their math workshops find that the effort yields phenomenal results: Learners are more engaged and successful as mathematicians.

Adding these four flavors of literacy instruction to your already full menu can appear daunting. For the purpose of this book, we teased them apart, yet in reality all aspects of literacy are interconnected; when we focus on one, it feeds the others. We need not explore all four at once, but just to have a go at one. Start something.

Start Something

As you reflect on what you might carry forward from this book into your own classroom, I invite you to be a conscientious consumer of ideas: What do your students need most? What will work for you? How can you adjust and own the instructional suggestions included in this text to best serve students in your setting? There is no wrong way; you need only begin, and these practices will take root and grow from there. Some suggestions:

- **Pick something.** Choose one thing—reflection writing, peer critique, reading mathematical masterworks—and make a commitment to weaving this practice throughout your instruction for at least one entire semester.

- **Start small.** Rather than feeling as though you have to stop the world so that you can make time for literacy, begin by fitting it in at intervals, in small doses, a few times a week, a few minutes at a time.

- **Level with students.** Explain why disciplinary literacy instruction is important. Ask them to participate in this experiment by gathering data on how the investment in literacy learning is serving their mathematical understanding.

- **Reflect.** With your classes, as well as with math teacher colleagues, an instructional coach, or your own self, take time to consider how this new emphasis is going. What is working? What more do you need?

- **Revise.** As you see opportunities for revisions to your literacy instruction, make them! Be more explicit with learners about your expectations; create new systems and structures to support this focus; be willing to let go of efforts that are not meeting students' needs.

- **Keep trying.** Don't give up. Change is difficult and takes time, yet as Carol Dweck (2006) reminds us, all can be won through effort.

Literacy instruction need not be "one more thing" that burdens you in your work with students, but rather can become "the thing" that glues their understanding together and supports learners in communicating their good ideas. This worthy challenge of literacy integration has the power to ignite interest, catalyze comprehension, and make mighty mathematical thinkers of all who enter our classrooms. As literate mathematicians, our graduates will find the doors to their futures wide open.

Appendix

Resources for Mathematics Enrichment

Books

These texts offer rich stories of mathematics in our world and could be excerpted for use with students.

How to Lie with Statistics, by Darrell Huff
Innumeracy: Mathematical Illiteracy and Its Consequences, by John Allen Paulos
The Joy of x: A Guided Tour of Math, from Zero to Infinity, by Steven Strogatz
The Mathematical Universe: An Alphabetical Journey through the Great Proofs, Problems and Personalities, by William Dunham
The Music of the Primes: Searching to Solve the Greatest Mystery in Mathematics, by Marcus du Sautoy
The Story of Science (three volumes), by Joy Hakim
Zero: The Biography of a Dangerous Idea, by Charles Seife

News Sources

These sources often feature articles and current events that can bring to light the relevance of math in our everyday world. Check them often to see what you find.

Alltop. "Math." http://math.alltop.com

CNN. *Light Years.* http://lightyears.blogs.cnn.com/category/on-earth/math/

New Scientist. http://www.newscientist.com

ProCon. http://www.procon.org

Science Friday. http://www.sciencefriday.com

Yummy Math. http://www.yummymath.com

Sources of Rich Problems

Each of these websites offers a range of rich math problems that offer fodder for reading, discourse, and writing about mathematics.

Achieve the Core. http://achievethecore.org

dy/dan. Blog, by Dan Meyer. http://blog.mrmeyer.com

Discovery Education. http://www.discoveryeducation.com

Illuminations. http://illuminations.nctm.org

Illustrative Mathematics. https://www.illustrativemathematics.org

Inside Mathematics. http://www.Insidemathematics.org

Mathalicious. http://www.mathalicious.com

Mathematics Vision Project. http://www.mathematicsvisionproject.org

NCTM. "Classroom Resources." http://www.nctm.org/resources/

Shell Centre for Mathematical Education. http://mathshell.org

Youcubed. http://youcubed.org

Bibliography

Abedi, J. "Standardized Achievement Tests and English Language Learners: Psychometrics Issues." *Educational Assessment* 8, no. 3 (2002): 231–57.

Abedi, J., C. Hofstetter, E. Baker, and C. Lord. *NAEP Math Performance and Test Accommodations: Interactions with Student Language Background.* Los Angeles: Center for the Study of Evaluation, National Center for Research on Evaluation, Standards, and Student Testing, Graduate School of Education and Information Studies, UCLA, 2001. http://www.cse.ucla.edu/products/reports/newTR536.pdf.

Abedi, J., and C. Lord. "The Language Factor in Mathematics Tests." *Applied Measurement in Education* 14, no. 3 (2001): 219–34.

Abedi, J., C. Lord, and C. Hofstetter. *Impact of Selected Background Variables on Students' NAEP Math Performance.* Los Angeles: Center for the Study of Evaluation, UCLA, 1998. http://www.cse.ucla.edu/products/Reports/TECH478.pdf.

Alliance for Excellent Education. *Confronting the Crisis: Federal Investments in State Birth-Through-Grade-Twelve Literacy Education.* Washington, D.C.: Alliance for Excellent Education, 2012. http://all4ed.org/press/new-report-offers-solutions-for-nations-literacy-crisis/.

Allen, Janet. *Words, Words, Words: Teaching Vocabulary in Grades 4–12.* Portland, Maine: Stenhouse, 1999.

Allington, Richard. "You Can't Learn Much from Books You Can't Read." *Educational Leadership* 60 (November 2002): 16–19.

Allington, Richard, ed. *Essential Readings on Struggling Learners.* N.p.: International Reading Association, 2010.

Allington, Richard L., and Peter H. Johnston. *Reading to Learn: Lessons from Exemplary Fourth-Grade Classrooms.* New York: Guilford, 2002.

Andrus, Miranda R., and Mary T. Roth. "Consequences of Inadequate Health Literacy." *Pharmacotherapy* 22, no. 3 (2002): 282–302.

August, Diane, Marie Carlo, Cheryl Dressler, and Catherine Snow. "The Critical Role of Vocabulary Development for English Language Learners." *Learning Disabilities Research and Practice* 20, no. 1 (2005): 50–57. doi:10.1111/j.1540-5826.2005.00120.x

Bangert-Drowns, R. L., M. M. Hurley, and B. Wilkinson. "The Effects of School-Based Writing-to-Learn Interventions on Academic Achievement: A Meta-Analysis." *Review of Educational Research* 74, no. 1 (2004): 29–58. doi:10.3102/00346543074001029

Baum, Sandy, Jennifer Ma, and Kathleen Payea. *Education Pays 2013: The Benefits of Higher Education for Individuals and Society.* Trends in Higher Education series. New York:

The College Board, 2013. http://trends.collegeboard.org/sites/default/files/education-pays-2013-full-report.pdf.

Beck, Isabel L., Margaret G. McKeown, and Linda Kucan. *Bringing Words to Life: Robust Vocabulary Instruction*. New York: Guilford, 2002.

Beers, Kylene. *When Kids Can't Read: What Teachers Can Do*. Portsmouth, N.H.: Heinemann, 2003.

Bennett, Samantha. *That Workshop Book*. Portsmouth, N.H.: Heinemann, 2007.

Biancarosa, Gina, and Catherine E. Snow. *Reading Next: A Vision for Action and Research in Middle and High School Literacy*. Washington, D.C.: Alliance for Excellent Education, 2004.

Blankenship, John. "Functional Illiteracy Continues to Grow, but There Is Help." *Register-Herald* (Beckley, W.V.), Nov. 5, 2013. http://www.register-herald.com/opinion/columns/functional-illiteracy-continues-to-grow-but-there-is-help/article_cd6059f3-43fe-5ecc-815b-af3946c3c597.html.

Boaler, Jo, and David Foster. "Raising Expectations and Achievement: The Impact of Wide Scale Mathematics Reform Giving All Students Access to High Quality Mathematics." 2014. http://www.sfusdmath.org/uploads/2/4/0/9/24098802/raising-expectations.pdf.

Borasi, R., M. Siegel, J. Fonzi, and C. F. Smith. "Using Transactional Reading Strategies to Support Sense-Making and Discussion in Mathematics Classrooms: An Exploratory Study." *Journal for Research in Mathematics Education* 29, no. 3 (1998): 275–305.

Britton, James. *Language and Learning*. Coral Gables, Fla.: University of Miami Press, 1970.

Bransford, John D., Ann L. Brown, and Rodney R. Cocking, eds. *How People Learn: Brain, Mind, Experience, and School*. Committee on Development in the Science of Learning, National Research Council. Washington, D.C.: National Academy Press, 2000.

Cazden, Courtney. *Classroom Discourse: The Language of Teaching and Learning*. 2nd ed. Portsmouth, N.H.: Heinemann, 2001.

Celedon-Pattichis, Sylvia, and Nora G. Ramirez. *Beyond Good Teaching: Advancing Mathematics Education for ELLs*. Reston, Va.: National Council of Teachers of Mathematics, 2012.

Cent, M. *The Achievement Gap: Colorado's Biggest (Education) Problem*. University of Colorado, n.d. http://www.ucdenver.edu/academics/colleges/SPA/BuechnerInstitute/Centers/CEPA/Publications/Documents/CEPA%20achievementgap.pdf.

Chapin, Suzanne H., Mary Catherine O'Connor, and Nancy Canavan Anderson. *Classroom Discussions: Using Math Talk to Help Students Learn, Grades K–6*. Sausalito, Calif.: Math Solutions, 2009.

Chomsky, Noam. *Syntactic Structures*. Boston: Mouton, 1957.

Clarke, D. J., A. Waywood, and M. Stephens. "Probing the Structure of Mathematical Writing." *Educational Studies in Mathematics* 25, no. 3 (1993): 235–50. doi:10.1007/BF01273863

Common Core State Standards Initiative (CCSSI). *Common Core State Standards (College- and Career-Readiness Standards and K–12 Standards in English Language Arts and Math)*. Washington, D.C.: National Governors Association Center for Best Practices and the Council of Chief State School Officers, 2010. http://www.corestandards.org.

"Counting Heads: A Breakthrough in Measuring the Knowledge Economy." *The Economist*, Aug. 28, 2004. http://www.economist.com/node/3127844.

Daniels, Harvey, Arthur Hyde, and Steven Zemelman. *Best Practice: Bringing Standards to Life*. Portsmouth, N.H.: Heinemann, 2012.

Daniels, Harvey, and Steven Zemelman. *Subjects Matter: Every Teacher's Guide to Content-Area Reading*. Portsmouth, N.H.: Heinemann, 2004.

Daniels, Harvey, Steven Zemelman, and Nancy Steineke. *Content-Area Writing: Every Teacher's Guide*. Portsmouth, N.H.: Heinemann, 2007.

DeWalt, D. A., N. D. Berkman, S. Sheridan, K. N. Lohr, and M. P. Pignone. "Literacy and Health Outcomes." *Journal of General Internal Medicine* 19, no. 12 (2004): 1228–39. doi:10.1111/j.1525-1497.2004.40153.x

Dewey, John. *How We Think*. Boston: D.C. Heath, 1910.

Draper, Roni Jo, Paul Broomhead, Amy P. Jensen, Jeffery D. Nokes, and Daniel Siebert, eds. *(Re)imagining Content-Area Literacy Instruction*. New York: Teachers College Press, 2010.

Duncan, G. J., C. J. Dowsett, A. Claessens, K. Magnuson, A. C. Huston, P. Klebanov, and J. Brooks-Gunn. "School Readiness and Later Achievement." *Developmental Psychology* 43, no. 6 (2007): 1428–46.

Dweck, Carol. *Mindset: The New Psychology of Success*. New York: Ballantine Books, 2006.

Gallagher, Kelly. "Reversing Readicide." *Educational Leadership* 67 (March 2010): 36–41.

Gifford, Margie, and Susan Gore. *The Effects of Focused Academic Vocabulary Instruction on Underperforming Math Students*. Alexandria, Va.: ASCD, 2008.

Graves, Donald. *Teachers and Students at Work*. Portsmouth, N.H.: Heinemann, 1983.

Harmon, J. M., W. B. Hedrick, and K. D. Wood. "Research on Vocabulary Instruction in the Content Areas: Implications for Struggling Readers." *Reading & Writing Quarterly* 21, no. 3 (2005): 261–80.

Hart, Betty, and Todd L. Risley. *Meaningful Differences in the Everyday Experience of Young American Children*. Baltimore: Paul H. Brookes, 1995.

Harvey, Stephanie, and Anne Goudvis. *Strategies That Work: Teaching Comprehension to Enhance Understanding*. Portland, Maine: Stenhouse, 2007.

Hattie, John. *Visible Learning: A Synthesis of Over 800 Meta-analyses Relating to Achievement*. London: Routledge, 2009.

Hiebert, James. *Making Sense: Teaching and Learning Mathematics with Understanding*. Portsmouth, N.H.: Heinemann, 1997.

Hiebert, James, James Stigler, and Alfred Manaster. "Mathematical Features of Lessons in the TIMSS Video Study." *ZDM* 31, no. 6 (1999): 196–201.

Hill, Jane D., and Kathleen M. Flynn. *Classroom Instruction That Works with English Language Learners*. Alexandria, Va.: ASCD, 2006.

Hoffer, Wendy Ward. *Science as Thinking: The Constants and Variables of Inquiry Teaching, Grades 5–10*. Portsmouth, N.H.: Heinemann, 2009.

———. *Minds on Mathematics: Using Math Workshop to Develop Deep Understanding in Grades 4–8*. Portsmouth, N.H.: Heinemann, 2012.

Hull, Ted H., Ruth Harbin Miles, and Don S. Balka. *The Common Core Mathematics Standards: Transforming Practice through Team Leadership*. Thousand Oaks, Calif.: Corwin, 2012.

Hyde, Arthur A. *Understanding Middle School Math: Cool Problems to Get Students Thinking and Connecting*. Portsmouth, N.H.: Heinemann, 2009.

Jackson, Julie, Sherry Tripp, and Kimberly Cox. *Interactive Word Walls: Transforming Content Vocabulary Instruction*. Science Scope. Arlington, Va.: National Science Teachers Association, 2011.

Jerald, C. D. *Identifying Potential Dropouts: Key Lessons for Building an Early Warning Data System—A Dual Agenda of High Standards and High Graduation Rates*. Washington, D.C.: Achieve, 2006. http://files.eric.ed.gov/fulltext/ED499838.pdf.

Johnston, Peter H. *Choice Words: How Our Language Affects Children's Learning*. Portland, Maine: Stenhouse, 2004.

———. *Opening Minds: Using Language to Change Lives*. Portland, Maine: Stenhouse, 2012.

Jurdak, M., and R. Abu Zein. "The Effect of Journal Writing on Achievement in and Attitudes toward Mathematics." *School Science and Mathematics* 98, no. 8 (1998): 412–19. doi:10.1111/j.1949-8594.1998.tb17433.x

Keene, Ellin Oliver. *To Understand*. Portsmouth, N.H.: Heinemann, 2008.

Keene, Ellin Oliver, and Susan Zimmermann. *Mosaic of Thought: The Power of Comprehension Strategy Instruction*. 2nd ed. Portsmouth, N.H.: Heinemann, 2007.

Kilpatrick, Jeremy, Jane Swafford, and Bradford Findell, eds. *Adding It Up: Helping Children Learn Mathematics*. Mathematics Learning Study Committee, Center for Education, Division of Behavioral and Social Sciences and Education, National Research Council. Washington, DC: National Academy Press, 2001.

Kittle, Penny. "Teaching the Writer's Craft." *Educational Leadership* 71 (April 2014): 34–39.

Klaus-Quinlan, Moker, and Sally Nathenson-Mejía. "Bridging Words and Worlds: Effective Instruction for Culturally and Linguistically Diverse Learners." Denver: Public Education & Business Coalition, 2010.

Kosanovich, M. L., D. K. Reed, and D. H. Miller. *Bringing Literacy Strategies into Content Instruction: Professional Learning for Secondary-Level Teachers*. Tallahassee: Center on Instruction, Florida Center for Reading Research, 2010. http://eric.ed.gov/?id=ED521883.

Langdon, David, George McKittrick, David Beede, Beethika Khan, and Mark Doms. *STEM: Good Jobs Now and for the Future*. Economics and Statistics Administration. ESA Issue Brief #03-11. Washington, D.C.: U.S. Department of Commerce, 2011. http://www.esa.doc.gov/reports/stem-good-jobs-now-and-future.

Levin, Henry, Clive Belfield, Peter Muennig, and Cecilia Rouse. *The Costs and Benefits of an Excellent Education for All of America's Children*. New York: Teachers' College, 2006. http://www3.nd.edu/~jwarlick/documents/Levin_Belfield_Muennig_Rouse.pdf.

Marzano, Robert J. *Building Background Knowledge for Academic Achievement: Research on What Works in Schools*. Alexandria, Va.: ASCD, 2004.

———. "Six Steps to Better Vocabulary Instruction." *Educational Leadership* 67, no. 1 (September 2009): 83–84.

Marzano, Robert, and Debra Pickering. *Building Academic Vocabulary: Teachers' Manual*. Alexandria, Va.: ASCD, 2005.

McConachie, Stephanie, Megan Hall, Lauren Resnick, Anita K. Raci, Victoria L. Bill, Jody Bintz, and Joseph A. Taylor. "Tasks, Text, and Talk: Literacy for All Subjects." *Educational Leadership* 64 (October 2006): 8–14.

McCullough, David. "The Danger of Historical Amnesia: A Conversation with Writer David McCullough." Interview by Bruce Cole. *Humanities* 23, no. 4 (July/August 2002).

http://www.neh.gov/humanities/2002/julyaugust/conversation/the-danger-historical-amnesia.

McNeill, Katherine L., and Joseph S. Krajcik. *Supporting Grade 5–8 Students in Constructing Explanations in Science: The Claim, Evidence, and Reasoning Framework for Talk and Writing.* Boston: Pearson, 2012.

Merisotis, J. P., and R. A. Phipps. "Remedial Education in Colleges and Universities: What's Really Going On?" *Review of Higher Education* 24, no. 1 (2000): 67–85. doi:10.1353/rhe.2000.0023

Merseth, Katherine. "How Old Is the Shepherd? An Essay about Mathematics Education." *Phi Delta Kappan* 74 (March 1993): 548–54.

Mezynski, K. "Issues Concerning the Acquisition of Knowledge: Effects of Vocabulary Training on Reading Comprehension." *Review of Educational Research* 53, no. 2 (Summer 1983): 253–79.

Michaels, Sarah, Mary Catherine O'Connor, Megan Williams Hall, and Lauren B. Resnick. *Accountable Talk Sourcebook: For Classroom Conversation That Works.* Pittsburgh: University of Pittsburgh, 2010.

Montelores Early Childhood Council. *Colorado's Children & Economy.* 2013. http://monteloresecc.org/community-members/colorados-children-economy/?doing_wp_cron=1425183233.0589361190795898437500.

Moore, David W., John E. Readence, and Robert J. Rickelman. "An Historical Exploration of Content Area Reading Instruction." *Reading Research Quarterly* 18, no. 4 (1983): 419–30.

Moschkovich, J. "A Situated and Sociocultural Perspective on Bilingual Mathematics Learners." *Mathematical Thinking and Learning* 4, nos. 2–3 (2002): 189–212. doi:10.1207/S15327833MTL04023_5

———. "Using Two Languages When Learning Mathematics." *Educational Studies in Mathematics* 64, no. 2 (2007): 121–44. doi:10.1007/s10649-005-9005-1

National Assessment Governing Board. *Mathematics Framework for the 2013 National Assessment of Educational Progress.* Washington, D.C.: National Assessment Governing Board, 2012. www.nagb.org/content/nagb/assets/documents/publications/frameworks/mathematics/2013-mathematics-framework.pdf.

National Center for Education Statistics. "Fast Facts." Institute of Education Sciences. Washington, D.C.: U.S. Department of Education, 2013. http://nces.ed.gov/fastfacts/display.asp?id=69.

———. "Reading and Mathematics Score Trends." Institute of Education Sciences. Washington, D.C.: U.S. Department of Education, 2015. http://nces.ed.gov/programs/coe/pdf/coe_cnj.pdf.

National Council of Teachers of English (NCTE). *The NCTE Definition of 21st Century Literacies.* Urbana, Ill.: NCTE, 2013. http://www.ncte.org/positions/statements/21stcentdefinition.

National Council of Teachers of Mathematics (NCTM). *Principles and Standards of School Mathematics.* Reston, Va.: NCTM, 2000.

———. *Principles to Actions: Ensuring Mathematical Success for All.* Reston, Va.: NCTM, 2014.

Organisation for Economic Co-operation and Development (OECD). *PISA 2009 Assessment Framework: Key Competencies in Reading, Mathematics and Science.* Paris: OECD Publishing, 2009.

Pearson, P. David, and Margaret Gallagher. *The Instruction of Reading Comprehension.* Technical Report no. 297 of Center for the Study of Reading. Champaign: University of Illinois, 1983.

Pearson, P. David, Laura R. Roehler, Janice A. Dole, and Gerald G. Duffy. "Developing Expertise in Reading Comprehension." *Contemporary Educational Psychology* 8, no. 3 (1992): 317–44.

Plaut, Suzanne, ed. *The Right to Literacy in Secondary Schools: Creating a Culture of Thinking.* New York: Teachers College Press, 2009.

ProLiteracy. "Growing Demand, Dwindling Resources." *The Crisis: The U.S. Crisis.* Syracuse, N.Y.: ProLiteracy, 2014. www.proliteracy.org/the-crisis/the-us-crisis.

Pugalee, D. K. "A Comparison of Verbal and Written Descriptions of Students' Problem Solving Processes." *Educational Studies in Mathematics* 55, nos. 1–3 (2004): 27–47.

Ray, Katie Wood. *Study Driven: A Framework for Planning Units of Study in the Writing Workshop.* Portsmouth, N.H.: Heinemann, 2006.

Reinhart, Steven. "Never Say Anything a Kid Can Say." *Mathematics Teaching in the Middle School* 5 (April 2000): 478–83.

Reinholz, Daniel L. "Peer-Assisted Reflection: A Design-Based Intervention for Improving Success in Calculus." Manuscript submitted for publication, 2014.

Ritchhart, Ron, Mark Church, and Karin Morrison. *Making Thinking Visible: How to Promote Engagement, Understanding, and Independence for All Learners.* San Francisco: Jossey-Bass, 2011.

Roosevelt, Theodore. *The Strenuous Life: Essays and Addresses.* New York: Century, 1900.

Rowe, M. "Wait Time: Slowing Down May Be a Way of Speeding Up!" *Journal of Teacher Education* 37, no. 1 (January 1986): 43–49.

Rubenstein, Rheta N. "Focused Strategies for Middle-Grades Mathematics Vocabulary Development." *Mathematics Teaching in the Middle School* 13 (November 2007): 200–207.

Schell, V. J. "Learning Partners: Reading and Mathematics." *Reading Teacher* 35, no. 5 (1982): 544–48.

Schleppegrell, M. J. "The Linguistic Challenges of Mathematics Teaching and Learning: A Research Review." *Reading & Writing Quarterly* 23, no. 2 (2007): 139–59.

Schoenfeld, Alan H., and Deborah Stipek. *Math Matters: Children's Mathematical Journeys Start Early.* Stanford, Calif.: Stanford University, 2011.

Schuster, Lainie, and Nancy Anderson. *Good Questions for Math Teaching, Grades 5–8: Why Ask Them and What to Ask.* Sausalito, Calif.: Math Solutions, 2005.

Senk, S. L., and D. R. Thompson. *Standards-Based School Mathematics Curricula: What Are They? What Do Students Learn?* Mahwah, N.J.: Lawrence Erlbaum, 2003.

Sfard, A. "When the Rules of Discourse Change, but Nobody Tells You: Making Sense of Mathematics Learning from a Cognitive Standpoint." *Journal of Learning Sciences* 16, no. 4 (2007): 567–615.

Shanahan, Timothy, and Cynthia Shanahan. "Teaching Disciplinary Literacy to Adolescents: Rethinking Content-Area Literacy." *Harvard Educational Review* 78 (Spring 2008): 40–59.

Siebert, Daniel, and Scott Hendrickson. "(Re)Imagining Literacies for Mathematics Class-rooms." In *(Re)Imagining Content-Area Literacy Instruction*, edited by Roni Jo Draper, Paul Broomhead, Amy Petersen Jensen, Jeffery D. Nokes, and Daniel Siebert, pp. 40–53. New York: Teachers College Press, 2010.

Siegel, Marjorie, R. Borasi, and C. Smith. "A Critical Review of Reading in Mathematics Instruction: The Need for a New Synthesis." In *Cognitive and Social Perspectives for Literacy Research and Instruction*, Thirty-eighth Yearbook of the National Reading Conference, edited by S. McCormick and J. Zutell, pp. 269–77. Chicago: National Reading Conference, 1989. http://files.eric.ed.gov/fulltext/ED301863.pdf.

Smith, Margaret S. "Reflections on Practice: Redefining Success in Mathematics Teaching and Learning." *Mathematics Teaching in the Middle School* 5 (February 2000): 378–82.

Spiegel, Alix. "Struggle for Smarts? How Eastern and Western Cultures Tackle Learning." *Morning Edition*, Nov. 12, 2012. National Public Radio.

Stahl, Steven, and Marilyn M. Fairbanks. "The Effects of Vocabulary Instruction: A Model-Based Meta-Analysis." *Review of Educational Research* 56, no. 1 (Spring 1986): 72–110.

Tennessee Department of Education. "Illuminating Student Thinking: Assessing and Advancing Questions." Nashville, Tenn.: Department of Education, 2014. http://www.tncore.org/sites/www/Uploads/files/K_2_training/Tab5a_Assess_Advance_Slides_NOTES.pdf.

Thompson, Denisse R., and Rheta N. Rubenstein. "Learning Mathematics Vocabulary: Potential Pitfalls and Instructional Strategies." *Mathematics Teacher* 93, no. 7 (October 2000): 568–74.

Tovani, Cris. *Do I Really Have to Teach Reading? Content Comprehension, Grades 6–12.* Portland, Maine: Stenhouse, 2004.

Turner, J. C., D. K. Meyer, C. Midgley, and H. Patrick. "Teacher Discourse and Sixth Graders' Reported Affect and Achievement Behaviors in Two High-Mastery/High-Performance Mathematics Classrooms." *Elementary School Journal* 103, no. 4 (2003): 357–82.

Vygotsky, L. "Interaction between Learning and Development." In *Mind and Society*, translated by M. Cole, pp. 79–91. Cambridge: Harvard University Press, 1978.

Waywood, A. "Journal Writing for Learning Mathematics." *For the Learning of Mathematics* 12, no. 2 (1992): 34–43.

Wilburne, J. M., and M. Napoli. "Connecting Mathematics and Literature: An Analysis of Pre-Service Elementary School Teachers' Changing Beliefs and Knowledge." *Issues in the Undergraduate Mathematics Preparation of School Teachers* 2 (2008). http://eric.ed.gov/?id=EJ835505.

Wittgenstein, Ludwig. *Tractatus Logico-Philosophicus*. London: Kegan Paul, 1922.

Woods, Baynard. "The Right to Think: Giving Adolescents the Skills to Make Sense of the World." In *The Right to Literacy in Secondary Schools: Creating a Culture of Thinking*, edited by Suzanne Plaut, pp. 13–24. New York: Teachers College Press, 2009.

Workforce Investment Act of 1998. Pub. L. No. 105-220–Aug. 7, 1998, 112 Stat. 936. http://www.doleta.gov/usworkforce/wia/wialaw.txt.

Zwiers, Jeffrey. *Building Academic Language: Essential Practices for Content Classrooms*. San Francisco: Jossey-Bass, 2006.

————. "Teacher Practice and Perspectives for Developing Academic Language." *International Journal of Applied Linguistics* 17, no. 1 (2007): 93–116.

Zwiers, Jeff, Susan O'Hara, and Robert Henry Pritchard. *Common Core Standards in Diverse Classrooms: Essential Practices for Developing Academic Language and Disciplinary Literacy.* Portland, Maine: Stenhouse, 2014.